BROWN GIRL ALMIGHTY

Copyright © 2024 Trinity Faith

All rights reserved. No portion of this book may be reproduced in any form without written permission from the publisher or author, except as permitted by U.S. copyright law. This publication is designed to provide accurate and authoritative information in regard to the subject matter covered.

Library of Congress: 2024913247

ISBN: 979-8-9899290-0-9

Illustrations by Cori Nelson | designwithcori@gmail.com
Front cover image by Dajzha Little | copaceticvision@gmail.com
Cover Model is Venissa Bansah | IG: @enabansah

First printing, 2024.

www.browngirlalmighty.com

BROWN GIRL ALMIGHTY

TRINITY

ILLUSTRATED BY CORI NELSON

CONTENTS

Author's Note   X

ACT I: BROWN

2	Heroes of our Own Stories
4	Protect the Crown
6	Red Lipstick
10	His-story
11	Stereotype
12	The Magician
16	Depression, my long lost lover
20	Inmate
24	Ode to My Hair
26	Gentrification
28	Lesson taught in Erasure
30	I want to know her name
34	This is what makes us girls
38	Million Dollar Houses
39	Indian Giver
40	Run me my money
42	Dreams & Nightmares
43	I've stopped watching TV
44	Keep hope alive
46	Intergenerational Parenting
48	Daddy Issues
50	A Child
51	Salvation

ACT II: GIRL

56	Puzzle Pieces
58	Hold Me Close
59	She Kisses Deep
60	Burn Baby Burn
62	The Florist and Her Flowers
63	06/11/2023
64	Manic Pixie Dream Girl
65	Brace Yourself
66	Captain Save A Hoe
68	Metaphors
69	Gravity Fucking Sucks
70	her hands
72	The Heart
76	with vengence, Trinity
78	Backtalk
79	Trust
80	I am a strong black woman
82	Scorpions
86	Masterpiece
88	the hopeless romantic turns heartless bitch
90	An Honest Poem
94	Battle
95	another statistic
96	Shots fired
100	Tokophobia
104	In praise of difficult women
108	A Happy Poem: Post Breakup
109	Things I cannot forget
110	The healer needs sleep
112	I am tired of dancing
114	My Mother Tongue

ACT III: ALMIGHTY

120	Take me home
121	I wish we could return to our true being
122	Pluto
126	Women Who Run With Wolves
128	The siren sings a "scary" song
129	ode to liberation
130	my yoni wants
132	Anatomy
134	she says I'm like water
136	the only time I've felt the holy ghost was at a concert
142	If looks could kill
144	Magical Women
148	Ripe
150	god I am
152	Being
154	Alternative Words for Sex
156	Eons
157	my ego is unbecoming
158	King Midas

Acknowledgments   162

Author's Note

I was 16 years old the first time I performed a poem in front of my high school. When Mrs. Stennis, my assistant principal, approached me afterward, she said, "Hey Trinity, I really liked your performance. You should write a book."

Her words never left my head.

She said it as though it was such a simple task. A thing she knew I was capable of achieving. And from that moment on, I started to compose this manuscript. Night after night. Poem after poem. Year after year, Brown Girl Almighty grew and shrunk and was lost and then found.

It's gone through 8 years of writing, 3 broken hard drives, 3 book covers, 12 denied submissions to literary agents and publishing houses, and only 6 people who have read her front to back.

This has taken a lot longer than 16 year old me expected, but I trust the universe with its divine timing.

Along with releasing this book, I am releasing many aspects of myself that I've held onto for so long. All of the stories, traumas, adventures, and heartbreaks that have shaped my becoming of self, just wanted to be expressed in this format.

Poetry is my everything and I am forever grateful for the people who have watered my garden.

To Mr. Leu for being the coolest poetry coach and always believing in my spirited personality.

To Jonathan for being a lifelong friend and down for all of my shenanigans.

To AB for expanding my creativity and Trei for showing me the beauty in everything. Gratitude to both of you for loving me unconditionally.

To Troy and Nasa for calling out my shadows and nurturing my metamorphosis.

To Hausson for all your poetic wisdom and Aries audacity.

To my mother, for showing me balance and saying yes to every hobby I wanted to try.

And to my father, for triggering transformation within me.

for my inner child

and all the words you yearned to say

ACT I
BROWN

If I were to mother a black child,
born from stardust may she be

The Heroes of Our Own Stories

As a child
dress up parties were my favorite activity.
I'd pick up every tulle dress
in every toy chest my friends and I had.
They told me I could be anyone I wanted,
but never said the princesses I dressed as
could be me.

I learned insecurity at an early age.
That whiteness was the epitome of beauty.
That my features were not worthy of a platform.
Even when black girls were represented
they were always too sassy.
Or loud.
Or invisible.
Marginalization introduced me to European beauty standards
before I could even spell my name.

At the age of seven,
I knew perms better than I knew my roots
and isn't that just like America?
To want us to forget where we came from.

Assimilation has always worked best
when the victim is taught to hate themselves.

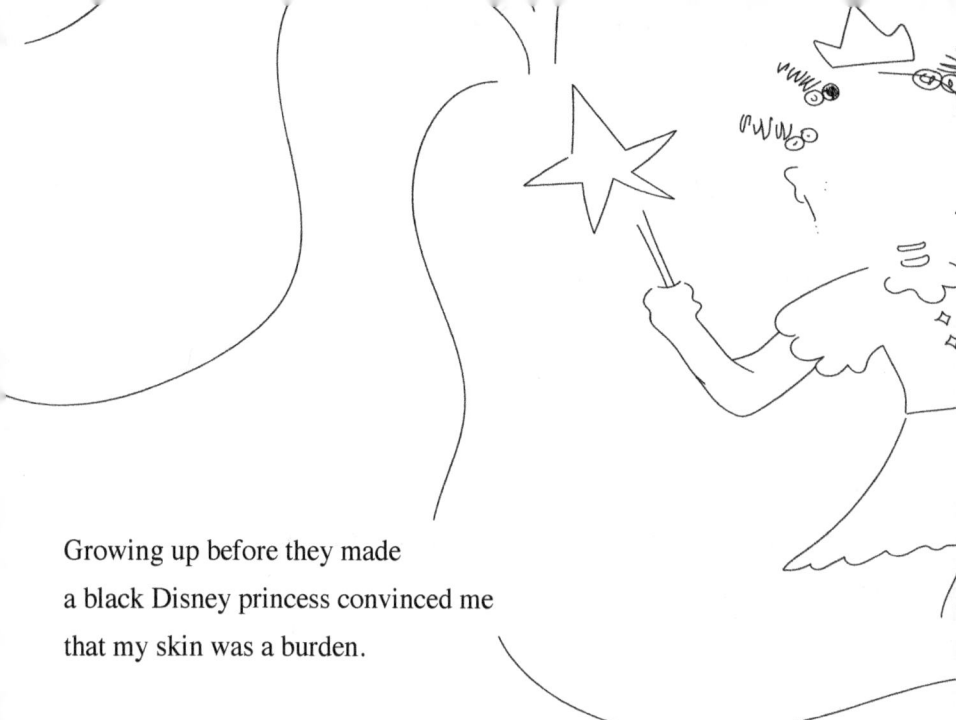

Growing up before they made
a black Disney princess convinced me
that my skin was a burden.

I should have never been able
to understand the weight of racism,
but it took Disney seventy-two years
to make a princess that looked like me.

One with brown skin, kinky hair, and full lips.

So now, I tell all the brown kids
who want to be princesses that,
of course, they can be Tiana.
But that they can also be their own.
Ones with bantu knots or cornrows or locs.
With dark skin or freckles or vitiligo.
That they can wear dresses or capes or tutus
and call themselves the heroes of their own stories.

Protect the Crown

Rest in peace to my hair that fell victim
to the creamy crack epidemic
I'm sorry the world tried white wash your boldness
before I could fall in love with it.

No matter what was done,
my hair was never good enough for them white folks...
Or them black folks.

My ends split
Roots thick
Shit still nappy
and I don't like the salon.
The air smells burnt and is thick with gossip
I am too young to have an opinion so I smile
when I'm told men ain't shit
that I have pretty eyelashes
to never trust a nigga til he lets you see his home.

My stylist flips between the news and old BET movies
She yanks the little curls I have left and
suffocates them under hot metal plates
The texture was drained from my crown and
no one ever explained the symbolism

That assimilation only works when insecurity has joined the party

That this was never my fight to begin with

That I was born a free woman in an enslaved society

and I have been picking up the pieces ever since.

My roots prevail

Ends split

Shit still nappy

but I have always been an untamable thing

There is no telling me to *Relax*

red lipstick

My father used to sell MAC cosmetics
out the trunk of his car

don't ask me how he did it.

I just knew it was a good day when he
let me pick through what he had
I remember doing this twice.

The last time, I spotted a Ruby Woo and knew I needed her bad
The Punky Brewster fun color-loving preteen in me
seen her bright red hue and loudly professed,
"That one!"

But my father refused
said some bullshit about how red wasn't
an appropriate color for a little girl
and all I could think
was how I didn't know a color
could be inappropriate for a little girl

What my father was telling me,
was that adults would be uncomfortable
seeing a 12-year-old in red lipstick
because it alludes to promiscuity

And how I dream of a world where my innocence
was nurtured longer than it was seen
as a game of who could take it first

One of the most frustrating aspects of growing up as a girl
were the disclaimers that came with it:
"Maybe you shouldn't do this."
"Maybe you shouldn't wear that."
I have a core memory of my uncle stealing shorts
out of my spend-the-night bag during the hot Georgia summers
and burning them when I wasn't looking

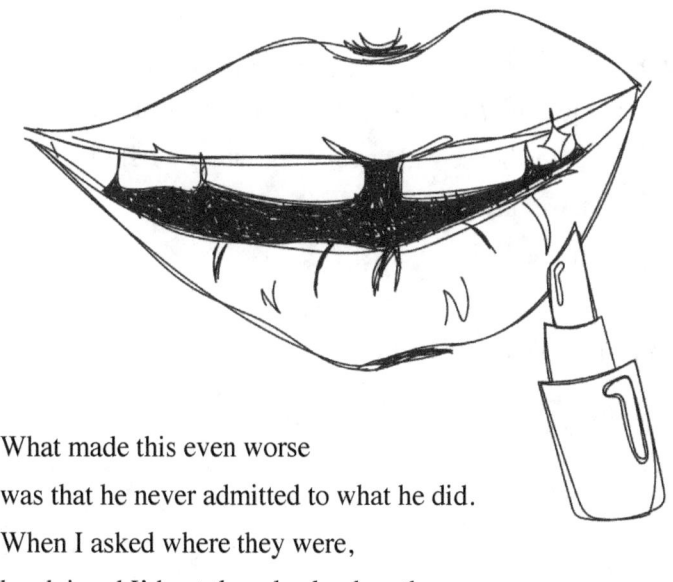

What made this even worse
was that he never admitted to what he did.
When I asked where they were,
he claimed I'd get them back when the summer was over.

I didn't know how inconvenient my existence was
or how distracting the development of my body could be.

When I look back
there were so many comments adults made about my appearance
and I did not understand what they were trying to say.

So I'd smile
and nod
maybe laugh
because I was taught to make others comfortable,
even when I was not

I don't remember the day that colorful leggings stopped being fun
and started making me concerned with how my body looked in them
When I couldn't leave the house without making sure my T-shirt
was long enough to cover my butt
I can guarantee that those were sad days

Ones I wouldn't want to remember anyway.

His·story

My ancestors have always had a tragic origin story
One bound in shackles or hung up in trees
I'd love to tell you a tale where we are
both the main characters and have a happy ending,
but that just seems like too much to ask.

My lessons have always begun in 1619.

Briefly mentions 400 years of slavery
and then pats white people on the back
for the little they did to end racism.

It doesn't acknowledge that the system was never abolished,
only rebranded.
Slavery birthed the prison industrial complex that
makes billions off the backs of niggas in chains.

It seems like all my people know is work.

When fields turn into factories
Slave catchers to sheriffs.
Sold fathers to absent fathers.
You'd have to benefit from this system so deeply to
not acknowledge the similarities.

Stereotype[1]

A widely held but fixed and oversimplified image or idea of a particular type of person or thing.

e.g., the officer handcuffs my best friend and asks, "You play ball, boy?"

---

[1] Collins Dictionary, Definition of 'stereotype,' Collins 2020.

i

The Magician

When I was a baby,
my father was great at helping my mother.
He used to do all kinds of things:
take care of me, clean the house, make dinner.
He was the whole nine.
So growing up,
I had this preconceived image of him.
He was the most helpful man I knew.
So helpful that when my mother wanted to leave,
He helped her put her shoes on.
He packed her bags.
He paid for the gas since being a single mother
is a long journey ahead.
See my father was a helpful man,
in front of everyone he needed to
believe that facade.
When my mother ran away from him
like he was a house lit up in flames
she never told me why or slandered his name.
Only made it clear that as I grew older,
I would see the man he really was.
I would see the tricks up his sleeve.
That the smoke and mirrors he hid the truth behind
wouldn't last for too long.

The magician did his final disappearing act when I was 15.

The Magician

I haven't spoken to him in three years,
it took me two to find out he ran away to Tennessee
and sometimes, I think I start to forget what he looks like.
But then I look in the mirror.
See how we are both alike in looks
and rage
and anger
and grudges
and how we do not forgive.
And this is why I love imagery,
for the way I can paint a pretty picture of him for you.
For the way he comes to life in my mouth
despite him being dead to me.

I can compare my father to a lot of things.

In one hand he is a gun.
A 44-semi automatic, his words fire when he is angry.
His mouth spews bullets when he is angry.
In another, he's a Bob the Builder ass nigga.
For the way he builds up relationships
only to tear them down,
and me?
I really am half the magic trick
and half the magician.

The assistant does what he commands.
Lowers herself into a box for the audience's entertainment.
Lets him poke and prod and jab while she smiles the whole time.
If she dares stop, the audience will lose interest.

And this is how my father saws women in half and
makes them feel forced to stay.

How he puts them in the spotlight
and expects them to love the attention
although it's killing them.
Although it's making a fool out of them.
But she still gives meaning to his performance.
Without her there wouldn't be a damn show in the first place.

My mother was literally giving my father pieces of herself,
and it still wasn't enough.
And I do this in relationships all the time.
I guess even bad traits are still passed down through blood.

See me...
I've got a couple of tricks up my sleeve.
I vanish a lot quicker than my father when things don't go my way.
I be flipping cards, levitating shit, walking on water.
Anything to distract people from the bad shit I do.

Anything to uphold my manic pixie dream girl illusion.

And I do believe in karma,
because all the bad I do to hide my pain
comes back to hurt me even more.

But I still be pulling niggas out of hats!

Making them do what I want in exchange for nothing.
Call it the sleight of hand,
call it a gimmick,
call it daddy issues.

I think the worst thing about my father being addicted to magic
is that he still does not have the power to go back and
fix his mistakes.

I'm supposed to love him.
I'm supposed to be his daughter, but it's hard
because it's like when he looks at me, he only sees my mama.

And what an illusion.
To be both his greatest creation of all,
and a reminder of everything he lost in the process.

Depression, my long lost lover

My ex best friend spoke of death as if he were an old lover
As if they'd spent late nights and early mornings together.
Laid underneath sheets of razor blades and
hosted long nights drunk off antifreeze.

She had the potential to bloom but was always
covered in too many thorns to do so

I remember her plans:
overdose on chemicals
jump off the roof
wrists to the blade

The day her family moved she was given
the room with a rooftop window.
If I was lucky, the nights she'd cry herself to sleep
wouldn't end with her jumping off it.
Instead, she'd sit outside and smoke cigarettes stolen
from the white boys in her neighborhood.

On good days
we'd watch them play basketball at the park.
We'd talk about John Green books and scroll Tumblr.
She told me "Helena" by My Chemical Romance
was the song she wanted to go out to

No matter what
the exit had to be aesthetic

Had to be true to our teen angst and rebellious nature

On bad days, we'd sit atop her roof while it rained
We'd play rock music loud as fuck
and take polaroids with our middle fingers up
Back then I tried to be the light in her darkness

I tried to be a good enough reason for her to stay but sometimes
being around her felt like the difference between life and death
I had never romanticized suicide as much
as I did when we were together
I tried everything in my power to keep her here
because I was under the impression that I could make her stay

My mother was never a fan of the bad girl
Said she was too much basket case and I
just looking for something to fix

One day
the truth came bubbling up my throat like bile
I told the counselor she was a threat to herself
and the bad girl vowed to never speak to me again

My ego spent so long trying to fix people
that a part of me was convinced
that whatever they did was my fault.

That I wasn't shoulder enough to cry on
or present enough when they relapsed
or that great at hiding the antifreeze.

I was 14
and in a constant state of worry
A mental institution was the last place I wanted her to end up
but I couldn't deal with her impending death
looming over my shoulder.

We don't speak anymore
but I hope she's better.

I hope she's somewhere living
the life we always dreamed about.

INMATE

I can't help but think that my cousin deserves to be in jail.

They say blood is thicker than water
but the relationships I've chosen
are stronger than the ones I was born into.

Maybe he deserves to be there because the family can't touch him.
Can't save him
Can't bribe his way out of prison
or sweep his sins under the rug
No amount of money
or pussy
will unbind him from the restraints he's placed on himself.

And I think that this is what he deserves,
but maybe I'm still bitter from the assault.

My cousin would have fed me to the wolves
and laughed as they devoured my body.
Shit, one time he actually did it.

I guess this is why manslaughter split in half is Man's Laughter
because I can still hear him.
Maybe it's from the first time,
or the second,
or the sixth.
Hell, I don't remember.

My brain automatically deletes traumatic experiences from my memory.

I'd say that this is helpful,
but what if I need to stand trial one day?

What if his sins catch up to him and I'm caught in the crossfire?

My paternal side will yell it isn't true
My maternal side will ask why I didn't say something sooner
and either way I am all anyone is looking at.

His charges read aggravated assault and possession
of a deadly weapon but I can assure you there's more than that.
Try sexual assault, larceny, pickpocketing, harassment, solicitation.
I'll never visit him in prison because seeing him locked up
won't make me feel any better.

When you've lived all of your life being the good to his bad,
Nobody thinks twice about you.
Nobody asks how you're doing and raises a red flag
when you always answer fine.
Nobody expects an answer other than fine
because being *seen* is one thing but to be acknowledged
is something completely out of this world.

The last time my dad's side has really *seen me* was years ago.

And that was only because I was in trouble and they
wanted to be in my business.
Because old black people love to be in young folks' business,
until it calls them out on their bullshit.

When my grandmother found out what my cousin did to me
she whipped both of us.

Do you see how I am always to blame?
How I am, still to this day, constantly questioning if shit is my fault.

Maybe they whooped me more to keep my mouth shut
than as a punishment.
Can't have this fucking up they image at the church.
Can't have a white stereotype plaguing this perfect black family.

I told my mom over a decade later what happened
and to my surprise, my grandparents never even told her.
Despite her anger, she says talk to them about it.
Call them on their birthday and over the holidays.
Schedule time to sit with them and bring up the animosity
hanging over our heads but,
If I wanted to hear a lecture… I'd go to class.

Who am I to expect a resolution from them?

If they acted like it didn't happen at age 6,
why would they acknowledge it now?

Honestly, this is not my problem and it never has been.
But if you ask them, they'll tell you otherwise.
Tell you that I went to college and couldn't call nobody.
That I came back from college and still couldn't call nobody.

See my family has this undeniable relationship with sexism
and grudges.
Maybe that's why nobody told me my grandad died.

Maybe in being a girl I'm always expected to have my shit together.

Maybe they've been setting my cousin up for this life sentence
his entire life.

Ode to my Hair

If I showed you a picture of me in elementary school,
my hair would have a million stories to tell

Chapter one would be about the relaxers.
About the way my curls learned to unravel themselves
for the sake of manageability.
Every few months
I had to retrain my new growth to fall in line
with the ones that came before it.

Chapter two would tell you about the pain.
About the way my scalp would burn the second
a relaxer was in for too long.
The neck cramps were inevitable.
My kitchen was always too thick.

Tender Headed was the nickname given to me
after I'd squirm under my Nana's grease covered fingers.
Most days, we were in a rush.
She'd say, "Sunday mornin service start in thirty minutes
and we ain't finna be late cuz of you."

If I showed you a picture of me in middle school,
you'd be confused.

This chapter only spoke dead ends and damaged hair.

I had color damage, heat damage, and my personal favorite;
don't know how to do no hair damage

Transitioning when my family only knew relaxers,
wigs, and the Dominican hair salon didn't do me any good.

When it wasn't in a ponytail
it was in braids from the African shop across from Popeyes.
They'd pull my scalp so hard that by the time I got out the chair
you could see the follicles sprouting out of my roots.

If I showed you a picture of me in high school
you would see the teen angst.

At many times my hair felt like
the only aspect of my life that I could control.
This chapter would tell you about the heartbreak
About the way I unlearned conformity and found impulsive
decisions to be the answer to all of my problems.

I got to know the men at my local barber shop very well
I befriended clippers and hair bleach
I made myself into an untouchable thing

One that was constantly learning her worth no matter how many
people tried to undermine how far she'd come.

Gentrification

I didn't question why all of the white kids slowly left
my neighborhood until I got to high school.
It was like each of my friends had been picked off
one by one and disappeared without a goodbye.
I heard they moved to cities like Kennesaw.
Or Alpharetta.
Or Woodstock.
All towns known for their large Caucasian populations
and expensive homes.

I remember my elementary school being diverse.
I was one out of four black kids in my class.
My friends and I would have playdates at parks
and count how many teeth we'd lost over the summer.
Every Halloween there was a bonfire in someone's backyard
and a sleepover at so and so's house.
So I wonder when my city stopped being good enough for
their parents.

I learned the term *white flight* in college.
It is when white people migrate out of racially diverse areas
and move into the suburbs.
Over the years, my city has undergone so much development
that my mother's house is now worth $160,000 more
than what she paid.

I learned the term *gentrification* in middle school.

When the apartments on Six Flags Drive were torn down.
When townhomes started to take their place.
When the property value skyrocketed the moment they built
a Chipotle.

Gentrification is when you renovate a community
until the people who live there can't afford it anymore.
And ain't that greed?
Didn't capitalism spread its legs and gift us another setback?

White folks think that just because I can sell my house for more money,
I don't care about the neighbor who lost hers.

I'd like to think that money doesn't make the world go 'round but what
am I to do when we put the value of paper over people?

I've seen a million men meet their fate at
raised property taxes and then home
renovators in the yard the next day.

So I wonder if my neighborhood
would be good enough

for them white folks now.

Lessons Taught in Erasure

My high school History teacher needs a lesson on pronouns

Every time we discuss slavery,
he uses the word, *we*, instead of the word, *they*
So instead of saying: "They enslaved, raped,
and beat all of the Africans."
He says, "We enslaved, raped, and beat all of the Africans."

This white man teaching a room full of Black and Brown kids
has forgotten that we do not share the blame with him.
It's almost like he's spent so long conditioning us
into complacency, that he has started to believe his own lies.

This white washed history serves as a pacifier
a whip to the back
a rope to the neck
anything to keep us in check.

It must be easy to forget the role your people played
when your school is 80% Black.
It must be easy to get caught up in a savior complex when
you spend all day listening to Ebonics.
I mean, it wasn't YOU who specifically stole our land
and pillaged our people.
You probably think you're righting the wrongs of your ancestors.

This is an advanced placement class,
so you must be doing all the right things!
This might as well be reparations!

You stamped a gold star on our heads and
tried to make us feel special.
We not like them other niggas.
We make this faulty education system look good.
We pay money to take tests that rarely give us anything in return.

Compliance is a disease that snakes its way through
black lineage and has historically kept us in order.
We have continuously been taught in erasure because
being brown in the classroom is synonymous to
being taught with our hands up.

For them, it is best when we are in a constant state of surrender
And even better when we are not aware of it.

I want to know her name

They found what was left of her in the woods in January 2012.
She was all bones.
Scattered amid the white snow.
I imagine that in her final moments, she stared at the sky.
Praying that a shooting star would wish her
out of an inevitable death.
I hope the sky was beautiful that night
I hope it shined just for her...

Did you know black girls are more likely to go missing
and still less likely to be found?

My obsession with true crime developed out of self protection.
I needed to know what to do if I was ever in their position.
Cuz black girls don't get amber alerts.
Or search parties.
Or names on headstones.

Did you know that in the country, you can still see the stars?

The night sky is a mirage of cosmic energy.
The speed of light travels beyond our comprehension
Light rays take thousands of years to dance across the galaxy
and if you blink for just one moment,
you will miss what was right in front of you.

She was right in front of you.

In the country town of Opelika, Alabama.
With a population of only 28,000 but no one knows her name.
If this were the 60's, you'd see her face on a milk carton.
Or not.
When black girls go missing they never get a cover story.
Just an unmarked grave and no one to claim as our own.

I'd tell you her name, but no one knows it.
And what a way to prove my point.
That when we go missing,
it is a privilege to have a name y'all can turn into a hashtag.

Sometimes my fear of not being able to protect our murdered girls,
triumphs my fear of becoming one.

Time has a funny way of ticking when you are constantly a target.

I was told not to write this poem as if I am a missing girl,
but isn't that the point?
That one minute I could be here and the next become a
Have you seen me? ad.

Do you know what it's like to lose your grip on reality?
To have it slip through your fingers like gravity?

Sometimes, my walk home feels like the difference
between life and death.
Sometimes, I get so cold I think my shadow has found
a warmer body to follow.
We've been searching for warmth in every living thing
we can get our hands on.
And isn't that just like a black girl!
To go missing without a trace.
To have people hashtag our names,
but never actually look for us.

This is What Makes Us Girls

The bad girl introduces me to Pierce the Veil in 8th grade.
I am outcast, bullied, a little insecure, but highly fashionable.
This is not a tale about depression,
it's about friendship.
About girl power being a canon event in all our storylines.
I refuse to tell you how our friendship was bad,
without also telling you how it was good.

At the start of 8th grade, we made vision boards out of our composition notebooks. Ripped bold words, popstars, and duck lips out of magazines and glued them down with Elmer's. Tiana was the only kid in class unfazed by what Vogue and Elle had to offer. She came to school the next day and her notebook was a mirage of teen angst. Black, white, gray, and red.
I didn't know her at the time, but I wanted to.

As an emerging poet, I was captivated by inspirational quotes. So when she showed me her notebook, I read with enthusiasm. Everything spoke to my heart about being a misfit, but I had never heard of any of the authors: Bring Me the Horizon, Sleeping with Sirens, Black Veil Brides, etc. Right before I could ask what this was, my eyes landed on the one: "Maybe I'll pretend right now, but I swear to God, I'm gonna change the world." - Pierce the Veil

My finger slams onto her notebook, "What is this?!"
"That's Pierce the Veil… It's a band. You should listen to them."

From that point on, Tiana and I were inseparable. We'd listen to Lana Del Rey and fantasize about moving to California. We'd talk about the boys we wanted to marry like Oli Sykes and Jaden Smith while crying over the ones who ignored us in high school. Tiana used to skip school to smoke cigarettes with the white kids while I'd take notes to fill her in on everything she missed.

After school, we'd take "Tumblr pictures" in tight skinny jeans and snapbacks and edit galaxies behind us.

2013 was a completely different world.

Tiana and I were obsessed with being in love and let the worst things influence how we viewed it. Evan Peters in season one of American Horror Story. Lana Del Rey's Ultraviolence album. Tumblr posts that said shit like:

> You can't love someone unless you love yourself
> first — bullshit.
> I have never loved myself.
> But you —
> Oh god, I loved you so much I forgot what
> hating myself felt like.
>
> My thoughts before I go to sleep. (via forsakenvows)
>
> 431,377 notes

Tiana taught me how to steal and I let the habit consume me for months. I'd slip whatever I could into my purse in any convenience store. Most of the stuff, I didn't even want. I was just looking for the thrill and maybe the attention? Almost everything I did was a cry for help, but I loved embodying a bad girl.

Here is where I could be loud and rambunctious in my own quiet and devious way. I could sneak high school flings into my bed when no one was home. Flirt with the people at work and fuck the pizza delivery guy.

Tiana inadvertently taught me how to lie. She was so bad at it that I became good. Saw exactly what not to do. So when my mom asked why my window screen was completely ripped open, it wasn't because I snuck out last night to fuck Justin in the backseat of his Honda Civic. "It's been ripping for a few months. The storm last night must've had its way."

Sometime between my first and second year of high school, Tiana and I's friendship started to fade. Once, she woke my mom up at 6:00 a.m. by accidentally knocking on my little brother's bedroom window. Tiana woke me up that morning in a manic state talking about the shit show that was her life. My mom's frustration grew. She didn't understand why I kept her around given how much trouble she was.

Our friendship was based on being teen girls who had all the emotions in the world but no one to relate to. We saw ourselves in each other and nurtured that for better and worse. I was short tempered, sexually repressed, and had daddy issues. She struggled with substance abuse, self harm, and raising all her siblings while trying to find ways to escape herself.

We loved each other despite.

Tiana gifted me a used dildo she'd stolen from her grandad on my 16th birthday. It was full of caffeine pills. That night, she brought weed to my Sweet 16 and smoked it with our classmates. My mom was livid. Vowed that the bad girl couldn't come around anymore. 3/4 of me agreed, but I still felt a unique connection with Tiana.

She couldn't have been that bad if she introduced
me to Pierce the Veil
If she kept me smiling after 3 years of on and off friendship.
And who's to say I wasn't as bad as her?
Perhaps my mother's disdain for Tiana was to disguise her
confusion for the teenager I'd become.
Because who am I if not a "bad girl" too?
I've sought thrills in the most dangerous places.
Alone at night in the streets of downtown Atlanta.
In the hands of strange men.
In rooms with women who hate themselves more than they hate me.

> In her book Communion, bell hooks says, "... women who suppress their own unique gifts in the interest of being dutiful daughters, wives
> and
> mothers are often filled with rage."

So ode to the bad girl for being an imperative part of my story.
For introducing me to new things to love about life.
For showing me girlhood in celebrity crushes, the color black, and "white people music."

For finding a lot to love in 13 year old me.

Million Dollar Houses

My mother and I ride through expensive neighborhoods
with million-dollar houses
She points out the ones with pools in the back
The ones that sit far from the road
The ones that look like three houses combined
The ones for sale...
I never know why she points out the ones for sale
Because while I am a fan of riding through
expensive neighborhoods
with million-dollar houses,
I don't like thinking of a life where we could afford one
We exist lower class.
I get free lunch at school because of low income
and rare child support checks.
Imagining a different life engulfed in
an expensive house and the luxuries that come with it
will make me jealous of what I do not have now.
I can only see the houses from behind the car window anyway.
I don't want to attend open houses
and pick out an imaginary bedroom that I'll never get to sleep in.
However,
we stop at a red light next to one that is for sale.
My mom looks at it
then pulls out the quick pick in the arm rest.
She shrugs, "Maybe we'll get lucky tonight."

Indian Giver[2]

An American expression used to describe a person who gives a gift and later wants it back.

i.e., they have always tried to reverse the roles of who was good and who was evil.

---
[2] Wikipedia, Indian giver, Wikipedia 2020.

run me my money!

Ask not what your country can do for you,
ask if your country still owes you some money
If it's as willing to donate to the descendants of slaves
the same way it will to the Notre Dame cathedral.
I've never seen that much money come together so fast
just to build up an 800-year-old church
What about every Black church that's gone up in flames
because of a white hand?
How do you force us into your religion
and then burn down the very place we pray to it in?

America was founded on hypocrisy
On little white lies
On ignoring problems until they carry a gun into a classroom.
And then justifying those problems under mental illness,
as if Black people don't suffer from psychological issues more
than whites.

It's crazy how you get into a position of power and
think you can do anything.
You are still building this country off pillage and martyrdom
while whining about slavery being oh so long ago.
Say that we can't possibly be suffering from 400 years'
of repercussions, while Black people are smothered under
this nation's thumb.

White people love acting like this is the greatest country in the world
and love forgetting who made it that way even more.

Their cheapest attempt at pacifying us
was trying to put Harriet Tubman on the 20 dollar bill.

Dollars are made of cotton.

And it's a tragedy
how the number one thing our ancestors fought to get away from
has become the least this country could do to apologize.

So ask yourself, has your country even gotten rid of
its biggest issues,
or has it just classified them under a different name?
Slavery turned prison system,
as if the system don't turn niggas into slaves
Ask if your country would fight for us,
the same way we've fought for it

and watch your answer, be no.

Dreams & Nightmares

Camryn tells me
for the past four nights
he's had this recurring nightmare.

In it,
his existence is made into a caricature
of the big black wolf.

In it,
he is seen as more beast than boy
and anything less than human.

Not even in sleep are we safe
The subconscious mind harbors our fears
and projects them in the dreamscape.

Irony is:
Society sees him as both
a big scary thing and
a small three fifths thing.

In this dream, he is portrayed as a trigger
As a target
As a threat by someone who only sees safety in a holster.

We live in a place where we are constantly looking over our shoulder
for fear of a sudden death that will come at no expense
to our murderer

I've Stopped Watching TV

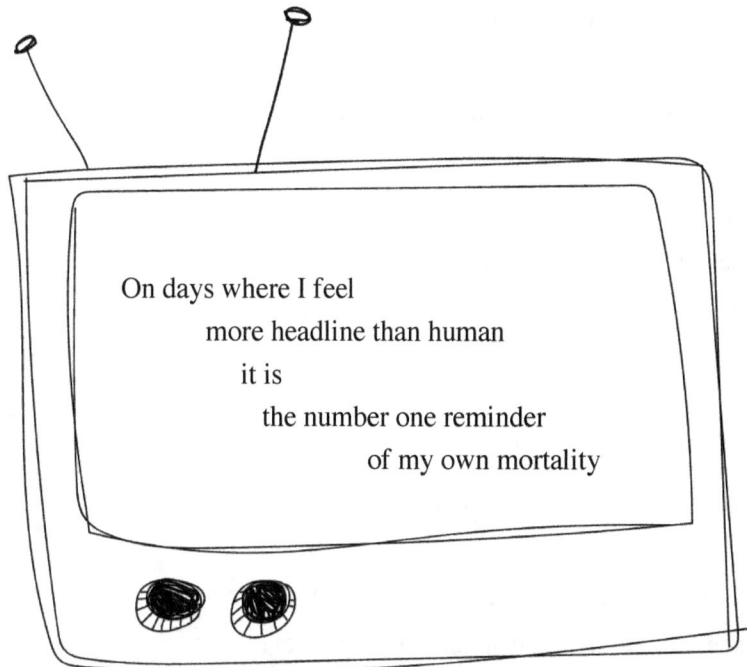

On days where I feel
more headline than human
it is
the number one reminder
of my own mortality

keep Hope alive

i don't believe in pharmaceuticals
but Hope says they make her feel pretty.
says, "feeling like a zombie is better than feeling like
i want to kill myself all the time."
and i can't help but miss the old her
even though i barely remember the old her.

all of my ex best friends have danced with the devil.
have run their fingers through his hair
and couldn't wait for the day he convinced them
to do the ultimate evil.

Hope used to joke about drinking bleach,
but i was never sure if she was kidding.

Tiana had a rooftop under her bedroom window
she used to fantasize about jumping off of.

i thought i could play savior to broken girls with
slits up their wrist and down their thighs.

this was no kink
no fetish
just programming.

14 years of seeing black women sacrifice themselves
for the sake of those they loved.

i had attracted so many people who needed so much healing,
i wrapped them in my arms and took on their burdens.

after years of cigarette butt burns and failed suicide attempts,
i'd had enough.
realized my first mistake was thinking
that i could stop them from wanting to die.

word around the bottle,
Hope is still tripping over her own apologies.
doctors still prescribing one issue out of many,
but she's stopped leaning on the pills to get her through the day.

the last time i spoke to her parents,
they claimed to not know what had happened.
said they kept their knees on the ground and palms glued together.
said the prayer must've started to take the pain away,
said one day they looked into her eyes
and saw a spark of Hope.

Intergenerational Parenting

Fear dictates most of our lives.
I see it in black mothers the most.

When they grab the switch,
it's because they were never taught
how to efficiently discipline their children.
All they know is how to beat and make bleed
their kids into submission.
They're just keeping up with the tradition.
Practicing what was passed down to them
because we still harbor our ancestors' fear.

Intergenerational trauma is inheriting
survival tactics we should've never needed
in the first place.

What's ironic is how the tables have turned.
We laugh at white people for their gentle parenting methods,
but refuse to talk to our parents because they beat us
with extension cords.

I wonder if we will forever suffer from the backends of slavery.

Unlearning trauma
and breaking generational curses
is one of the hardest things to do,
but the payoff is immaculate.

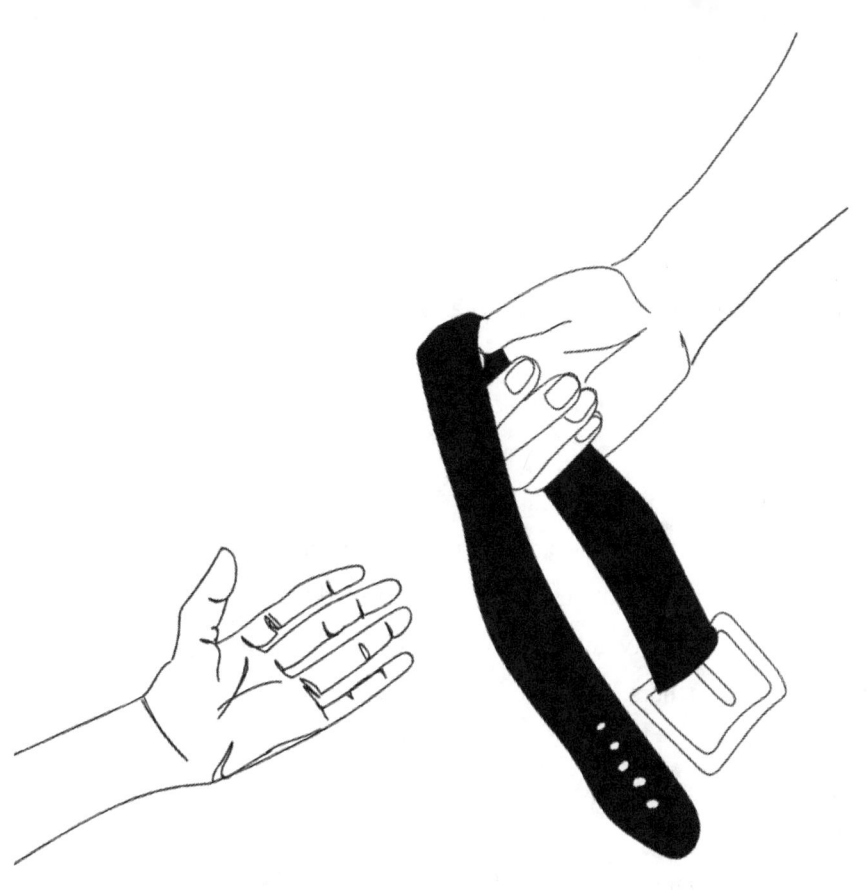

Fear only exists if we allow it to.
And by choosing a softer path, we choose ourselves.
We choose everyone that came before
and all who will come after.

And isn't that enough?

Daddy Issues

Many studies show
that girls raised without their fathers
tend to be more promiscuous at an early age.

Upon reading this, my heart sunk.
I've never related to a statistic more.

I've fumbled for the hands of many men in the dark.
Bent over middle school desks when they passed by.
Snuck kisses in empty hallways and in the back of the library.
Under gym bleachers.
In movie theaters.
Behind the Boys and Girls Club.

Nothing excited me more than a boy eager under my sheets.
I wanted them to stick their hands in my pants for the thrill.
I needed them to see me naked.
I needed them to see me legs spread and pleading.
Begging for their attention and dripping wet.

My family always acted like this was my fault.
Not once did anyone look to my father.
Not even when I was caught naked in the hands of a boy at 12.
All I remember is wanting him so bad in ways
I did not know how to express.

Both of them.
My father and the boy.

They say present fathers instill independence in their daughters
and the comfort in knowing that at least one man loves them deeply.
These girls don't look to penis for validation.
Don't "Act Like a Woman, Think Like a Man" their way into love.

I had to Father myself through heartbreak and headache.
Through feelings of unworthiness and
the trials of being a strong black woman.

There weren't many places I could rest my perfectionism
or men I could ask for advice.

I spent a lot of time worried about how others would view my path.
I didn't want to be fast or loud or unladylike.
I was made to believe that likability was the key to success,
but all it taught me was how to deny my truth.

So you can save your judgment.

My uncle shows me a picture of my father shortly after I was born.

He asks, "What do you see?"

I say, "A child."

Salvation

I've been waiting on a man to come and
save me from myself

Deliver me the pleasure I've been searching for
in the backseats of Honda Civics
and in public restrooms

Never good enough to rendezvous in bed
and certainly not to wake up next to you

Rob says, "That'd create too much attachment."

Yes

Me waking up next to your pretty face will kill us quicker than
you fucking me raw on the first night

I am tired of men
but I want them so badly

I want them to want me
so badly.

ACT II
GIRL

I used to think the world was beautiful...
until it wasn't.

it was like the curtain had fallen amid act two and suddenly

everything was upside down

Puzzle Pieces

I remember the first time I kissed a girl.
It was just like the movies said it'd be.
The beginning of senior year.
The heat of summer preparing for its transition to fall.
You slowly walked closer to me
until my back was pinned against the brick wall.
If I hadn't been so wrapped up in you,
I would've been self-conscious that we were standing
where any passerby could see us.
But your scent caught all of my attention.
Your hands kept grabbing my waist.
Your voice got softer the more you leaned in
and I exhaled out every ounce of worry
when your lips finally met mine.
When we kissed for the first time,
it was like finding something that was missing.
Like unlocking a character in a video game.
In that moment,
I was convinced
that there was no such thing
as having enough of you.
I vowed to bring you everywhere.
Our definition of fun
was getting high and making out
in the back of my best friend's SUV.
After we'd hotbox his car, I'd take your hand
and make you dance with me to "Teenage Fever" by Drake.

Once, I was so high that I closed my eyes
and when I opened them,
we were a mile away from where we started.
I was a romantic before all of this
but you made me put *hopeless* in front of it.
You made me forget the hurt.
You made me put my faith in you.

hold me close

if i could,
i would map out the shape of my love for her
in the scratches i leave on her back

i would tell her every thought that runs
through my mind when i see her
or how i changed her ringtone
so i know when she texts me

the last time i cried,
she unbuttoned my shirt
to trail kisses down my chest
and i was resurrected every time
her lips touched my skin

i believe that her lips will cure all my problems
that every time she makes me lose my breath,
all i'll need is for her to hold me close and suddenly,
breathing will become all i've ever known

she kisses deep.
not like she is the drought and i am water

but like she needs me to love her
because she cannot love herself.

burn baby burn

My grandma is bold enough to claim that she can *fix* me.
Like I am a dog
Something beneath her and her christian values.
Never worthy of a spot on the pulpit,
but just right to smile in pictures
and make everyone jealous.

The most perfect families always have the biggest secrets.

I never cared to come out.
Straight people don't have to, so why should I?
I spent years seeking solace in immature boys
so when I found it in a girl,
it was the purest of experiences.

Exploring the curves of our bodies against each other.
Kissing behind buildings and getting high to Kehlani
Tongues and fingers in all the right places.
We were like aliens exploring a new planet.
Seeking home in one another.
A space where we could finally take a deep breath.

My family won't tell me that they don't agree with my *"lifestyle,"*
but they will turn away from the TV when two girls kiss.
Passive aggression is the whispers at my graduation party.

It's my mom being asked, "Why you let her do that?"
when I'm not around.

My family is full of hypocrites who have secrets.
No one is willing to look in the mirror,
because they're too busy pointing a finger.
They're going to tell me that I'm wrong
That they don't want to see me go to hell.

But what if I'm not afraid to burn
if it means I'll burn with you?

Your eyes are portals to another dimension
A place where I am *seen*
heard
safe
with no second guesses.

I'd choose burning for an eternity if it means
I get to live in love.

So may my death be revered
May my funeral be a momentous occasion
There are no tears to be shed over a life lived
in love.

May I see you
the next incarnation.

The Florist & Her Flowers

When she kisses me
it feels like I am the flower
freshly plucked from the soil
and she is the florist trying to keep me alive.
If I hadn't spent most of the relationship
with rose-colored glasses on,
I would have questioned why she'd taken me
out of my environment sooner.
My first love was manipulative.
She'd place me in a pot
and then leave me to die on a windowsill.
I've grown to have a bad memory because of the trauma.
I'd watch her walk in and out so many times
it felt like I was the one getting my hands dirty.
She loved to watch me wilt,
but every time I bloomed without her, she'd be angry.
Defensive.
Jealous.
I spent four seasons
transitioning for her
and in the end,

it still wasn't enough.

06/11/2023

Today is my birthday.
And every year,
I wonder what my father thinks about that.

I imagine that if I had a daughter I didn't speak to,
I'd cringe during her birth month,
distract myself the week prior,
and avoid the calendar the day of.

I'd disguise the shame bubbling up my throat as indifference and
swallow my pride with something bitter
Hard.
Forgetful.

I couldn't imagine having a daughter that I didn't speak to.
I couldn't imagine telling her about how mean and hurtful
the world can be, and then abandoning her the second she
doesn't agree with me.

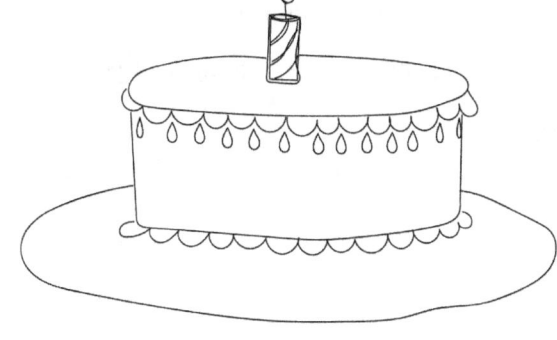

My father was the first man who made me feel like a
Manic Pixie Dream Girl

Manic Pixie Dream Girl[3]

A stock character in films. [She] seems to exist only to provide spiritual or mystical help to the protagonist. The MPDG has no discernible inner life. Instead, her central purpose is to provide the protagonist with important life lessons.

    i.e., Ramona Flowers in "Scott Pilgrim Versus the World"
    Summer in "500 Days of Summer"
    Margo Roth Spiegleman in "Paper Towns"
    Sam in "The Perks of Being a Wallflower"

I am the one who will get hurt to advance your plot.
Use me.
Abuse me.
It doesn't matter.
I was created for the betterment of you.

---

[3] Wikipedia, Manic Pixie Dream Girl, Wikipedia 2023

Brace Yourself

I did not want to prepare for the heartbreak,
but you started to change.

Walking the halls like you've got
somewhere to be and
someone to see.

You wouldn't kiss me on the lips anymore,
It had been so long,

I'd
        forgotten
                what

                        you

                              taste

                                      like.

Captain Save-a-Hoe

In various stages of my life
I've wanted to be the savior in someone else's story

Give me the credit of saving you from yourself
Maybe it will mean that I am worth something

This society told me my purpose is in what I do
and how much money I make from doing it

How do I make people feel?
Is it good?
Is it worthy of a standing ovation?

They don't teach you about self-worth in school
or emphasize that it comes from within
So excuse me for trying to find myself
amongst compliance and submission

I've been making up for lost lessons
Unlearning teachings that have smuggled their way
into my subconscious

And this work is tiring
So very tiring

Metaphors

The only way I can describe
    my feelings
        are through metaphors

I do not say, "I am sad."
I say, *I am the dripping faucet.*
The crying clouds.
The storm inside of us all.

I do not say, "I am impatient."
I say, *I am the sand formed*
from disintegrated rocks
forever waiting on my chance
to be whole
again.

gravity fucking sucks

I am losing you.

You are slipping
directly through my fingers
and I curse the fact
that I cannot control gravity
and make you stop.

her hands

i didn't realized that i didn't want my lover,
until my hands were pried away from hers
and we were taken 300 miles apart.

high school love could have been the death of me.

it was the second time i'd come face to face with how hard i fall.
back then it was all codependency and fear.
going to different schools was the proper end to our entanglement,
so of course i held on tighter.

the thought of you with other women did not sit well with my ego.
i was still addicted to your abuse.
to the struggle that was loving you.

i would have winced through the pain if it meant
i'd still take up some of your time.
if it meant i'd still get to feel your fingers inside of me.

which makes me question what i thought i was missing out on
in the first place?

there are millions of fingers that perform better than yours.
tens of thousands of arms to fall into and mouths to kiss.

months passed and i'd still masturbate at the thought of you.

and it isn't even that you touched me in the holiest of ways
maybe it's the fact that you didn't,
that I wanted you to so badly.

my ego likes control
could do without the change
and maybe this was just one of her games.

what trickery i have found myself in
time and time again

to lose a love that never even resonated within.

The Heart

There are three main theories for where the heart symbol comes from.

The first says it derives from the African plant *Silphium*.
An aphrodisiac that acts as a contraceptive,
seasoning, and medicine.
Legend to be so valuable that Julius Caesar
hid 15,000 pounds before its extinction.
It was used as a trade for goods
and services.
Put on coins.
Sold as the idea of love to peasants
who didn't have anything but the
promise of holy matrimony.

The second comes from Aristotle.
Before autopsies, he claimed that the
human heart had 3 chambers instead of 2.
The drawing he made looks like the
emoji we know today.

The third comes from two anatomical human hearts
being stitched together.
This theory was recreated for visual purposes a few years ago.
In the picture, two hearts have been sewn together.
Their left ventricles made into one.
Their aortas shaved down.
Veins and arteries snipped away and so far,
this has been my favorite theory.

I was 10 when I crowned myself *Hopeless Romantic*.
Swooned at the sight of chivalry and fell asleep to passionate fantasies.
Made wedding vision boards and said, "That's my dress!"
to every gown in a bridal magazine.

Throughout my idolization of love,
I misplaced what it meant to love myself.
Cared about others perception more than
my own, and cut myself in half
to make another feel whole.

In one hand, I think this theory is
beautiful, but in another, it is not.

Some of us would rather be pierced
with a needle and thread than to find a
love that doesn't hurt.
So is this what they mean when they say
to mend a broken heart?

For so long
I relied on someone to make me feel whole,
but what does that say about me?

If I leave my validation up to others,
do I stop standing for myself?
Am I not complete on my own?

Abusive relationships taught me that there's nothing
I can do for someone until they're strong enough to do for themselves.

So I think it's time to take matters into my own hands
To stop limiting myself for the sake of others.
To stop seeking long term answers out of temporary people

The world tells me I need someone, but I think the fuck not.
I think the theories are bullshit.
I think Aristotle can go to hell.

████,

would it be a stretch to say you killed me?
that i literally died of heartbreak
spent a lifetime trying to make this work
and my only reward was dying in your arms

i know i have a flair for the dramatic
but you deserve every ounce of my theatrics

i was left bloody and battered
in the middle of the road
your knife in my chest
and the last thing I could see
was your initials engraved in the handle

caress me like a holster
hold me like a grudge
look me in the eyes when you lie to me

tell me you're the problem and then tell everyone else it is me

What is it like to pray for a Godly woman?
soft like silk
sweet like fruit
Who shines like gold,
but not be able to stand the heat?

███,

you are not the first man who's stared into my innocent face,
knowing he was about to break my heart
I pity fools like you

How do you play God?

Feel the ebbs and flows of her being
Backstroke in her rivers
Dive deep into her ocean
Penetrate her psyche
and then play with her intuition

All the softness I had for you was lost in the end times
Our own personal armageddon

I deserve to be loved without an unreasonable doubt
and I forgot that truth when we were together.
So fuck you, ███

with vengeance,
Trinity

My father once used the fact that I didn't know him as a reason for why I shouldn't talk back to him.

I responded, "That's the problem."

I am so used to people only loving me for my body.

How am I to trust you'll be any different?

I am a strong black woman

not by choice
but because I was forced into this position.
I've worn hyper-independence around
my neck like a gold medal.
Prided myself on not needing you or any man
who thinks he can bring something to my table.
I've got shame
pride
guilt
and right now they all look like the exact same thing.

My father abandoned me
My uncles abandoned me
My grandfathers abandoned me
and I've spent my entire life unpacking the trauma.

On one hand, I've made myself into an Untouchable thing.
Spent years building this resume and achieving these accolades.
Everywhere I go people recognize my face.
On the other hand, I'm asking myself,
why don't you love me?
Didn't I do everything right?

I've got my own house
My own car
Built my career from the ground up
So why am I not good enough?

I've worn this pride so long it has become a noose around my neck.

To be the first daughter of a single black mother is to be martyr.

I've felt the weight of trying to be everything for everyone my entire life.

Spent the loneliest days accepting advice
from those unfit to give it to me.
They said I needed to be prim and proper
On time
Likable
Hard-working
but now,
I've been painting my own picture of how I want my life to look,
and with that comes unlearning *everything*.

So, you see,
I am a strong black woman,
but not in that order.
I am *being* before I am black woman
I am *kind* before I am strong
I am *funny* before I am sacrifice

Scorpion
circa 2018

I know the things I do
I know when I'm giving too much
to someone who doesn't deserve it
Or making excuses
Or playing backseat in a story
I'm supposed to be the main character in.

I know exactly what my problems are.
I know I tend to write about the abuse
because sometimes I think the abuse is all I am
Like that's the most interesting thing about me.
Like the fact that I escaped death in the nick of time
is something that'll convince someone I'm worthy of theirs.

I want to write about something else,
but I've got attachment issues.
Got *daddy stayed gone for so long a part of me just wished he'd stayed gone* issues.

I bet that's what keeps me loving all the wrong people and not myself.
I've waited so long for someone to love me for me and not leave
My attachment issues make me pull people too close and push them far away.

But maybe that's the Gemini in me.
I take from all the right people and give to the wrong ones.
Safe to say, I've got bad judgment.

Safe to say that my attachment issues make it hard
for me to forgive and forget.
A part of me thinks if I love someone enough,
I'll learn how to love myself through them.
But then again,

I'm terrified of love.
Because the last time I was trapped in it,
the girl pursued me.
Held me down so I couldn't cry for help.
Stung my heart like I was her prey
but then again,

she was a Scorpio.

And did you know that scorpions can live for a year with no food?
Did you know that's how long she had been feasting on me for?

When depression swallowed her coping mechanisms,
it left me to pick up the little that was left of her.

She was like a small child learning how to do things for the first time.

I had to reteach her basic shit like,
how to get off my hip and go make friends.
How not to throw a tantrum every time I said no.
How to communicate.

When I'd have to piece together her sentences,
it was like writing poetry for the both of us.
And my god,

I can barely carry the weight of my own feelings,
so how the hell was I to carry hers too?

She made me impatient.
Made me hurt so bad I wanted to die
When she yelled at me for the 100th time,
she said she didn't understand why I stayed after
everything she put me through.
Said that it was stupid to love someone
who wasn't in the position to love you back...

But isn't this the only way I've learned how to love?
With a hand around my throat
With my tears soaking the pillow
With all my hard work wasted on a not shit bitch
It's like I be working on people longer than they
be working on themselves.

And I wonder what it would look like
if I put all that energy into myself.

My mama says, ain't nobody gon be there for me more than me.
And I try to remember that.
Try not to be so selfish.
Go through phases where it feels like I've got scissors for hands
with the way I be cutting niggas off.

But maybe it's the wrong niggas I'm cutting off,
because I'm still in this position.
Still feeling sorry for the girl who abused me.

And look at that,
how I still end up writing about the abuse…

like it's all I am

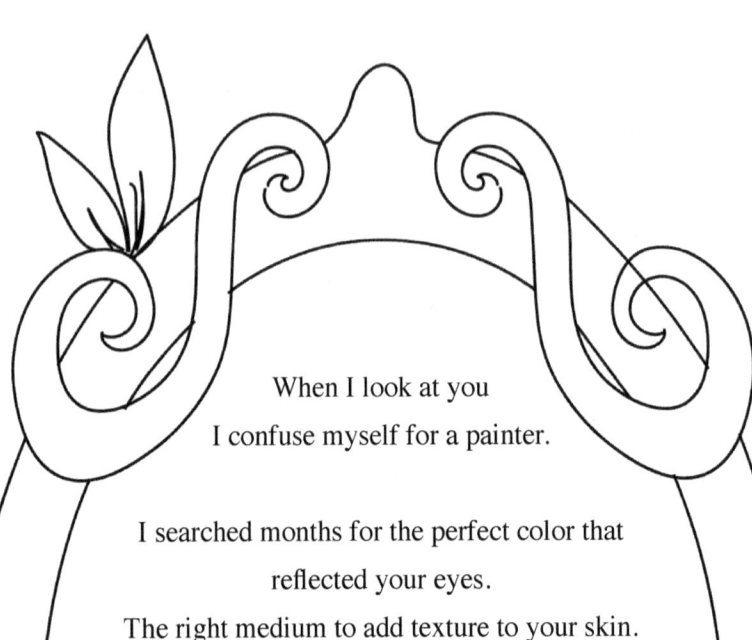

When I look at you
I confuse myself for a painter.

I searched months for the perfect color that
reflected your eyes.
The right medium to add texture to your skin.
I wanted to make sure that my details stood out.

Had to perfect the goosebumps that rise every
time I hold you just right.
Or the hairs that stand on the back of your neck
every time I come close to you.

I figure you owe me this accreditation.
I went through hell to make
you a better version of yourself.

The least you could do is
give me a round of applause.

I put elbow grease into your deficiencies.
Picked you up when you were down.
Answered the phone every 3am
and cried when you were hurt.

It took me forever to realize that I am not
the artist who crafted you out of a blank canvas,
or the poet who wrote you into existence.

Which is to say,
it is not my job to help you
when you can't even help yourself.

how the hopeless romantic turns heartless bitch

i've learned that abusers love to play victim
love to play the blame game
love making me cry,
because when i do it
i look more *fuckable* to her.
maybe that's why i always am

because now i think crying is what I know best.
and maybe this is my fault
because i put these niggas on a pedestal
let them forget where they came from
like they didn't find a way to love themselves through me
like i wasn't their hype man until they stopped relying on me
like they didn't get cocky through my validation
and leave me when they didn't need it anymore

ill be the first to admit that i tend to give these niggas
too much credit.
i told the girl i couldn't sleep without her on the phone
so she hung up and didn't call back.
i told the girl i wanted to take things to the next level
and she told me she'd been dating my friend.

i keep putting my all into people who don't reciprocate my energy.
and this is the how the hopeless romantic turns heartless bitch.

turns too scared to trust anyone else,
hell she can't even trust herself.

too scared her desire for love will get her caught
in another heartbreak.

caught in another fling with a girl who doesn't love herself
enough to love her back.

i told her, you can't complain about people leaving when
you push them away.

she left me many times
only to come back on her knees
saying that it was always my love that did her any good.
but now, its over
and I hate her
because she is both the reason i stopped writing
and the reason i can't stop.

but i can't wait for the day that i write poetry about someone else
and let that someone else be me.

An Honest Poem
circa 2017

When I introduce myself I say, "Hi, I go by Rin."
People normally ask me to repeat myself so I say,
"Wren, like the bird."
Because there's a bird named Wren,
which is fitting because we're both small.
For 7 years, I was under the assumption that I was 4' 11",
but after shaving my head I am 4' 10 ½".
So let's jump into it.

Hi, my name's Rin, I am 17 and for a pessimist,
I'm pretty optimistic.
I started kissing girls one wet day in August a few years ago
and I haven't looked back since.
I think being straight was my phase.

I have a strong bias against Scorpios and
people whose names start with J.
That's because there was Jane, Jazmin, Jessica - you get the point.

I've learned that my words hurt way more than my actions
because people love my poetry, until it's about them.
They be like, "Spit yo truth sis! But not about the shit
I put you through."

However, my ex says she never truly knows what I'm thinking,
until I read her a poem.

That's because she loved being the center of my world
and wasting my time
Although I have a lot of opinions,
I tend to sugar coat them when I'm in love.
I call this compromise.
I do not sugar coat my poetry.
She put me through a year's worth of trauma
and it took me leaving for her to realize her faults.

My mom says I do not deserve the projects I've been dealt.
A hobby of mine is giving great advice I don't take,
but doesn't everyone?

I also enjoy daydreaming, contradicting myself,
and trying to "make it" so I can drop out of college.
I wanna write until my fingers break.

I don't do snapchat streaks because they're too much commitment
For my 16th birthday, my mom got me a puppy and
I gave it right back
Told her I was incapable of taking care of anything
that wasn't myself.
This is still very true and the reason I don't want kids.

Sometimes, I want to escape.
On days where the sky looks like cotton candy,
I want to stick my head out the window and taste it.

I guess I don't look up enough.

I wonder how much the sky goes unnoticed
because we're stuck with our heads to the ground.
I've experienced loving and losing at the exact same time
and have not stopped writing about it since.
I often think to myself, *Damn, I go through a lot of emotional
trauma, but at least the poem is gonna be fire.*

Whenever I explain my sadness, people are like, "Who hurt you?!"
And I'm like, "Bitch, everybody!"

Lately, I've been learning how to let go in little ways
I donated a shit ton of clothes and finally threw away that
dollar lipgloss I'd been holding onto for 2 months.
It had a millimeter of gloss left in it
I had to hold the bottle right side up so it could slowly
slide down the tube,
but then I asked myself, *Why am I waiting?*
Why am I holding onto things that don't serve my purpose anymore?

I love contradicting myself!
Like starting a new poem and saying I won't mention you,
but then the whole poem is about you.
Whether it be in twisted metaphors or complicated similes,
I am always writing.

I told the girl that my favorite color is yellow
and she says she's never heard that one before.
A part of me feels special.

Like I'm the manic pixie dream girl that will solve all her problems.
Like I have none of my own.
What I really wanna say is that my mental health is not up to par.
What I end up saying is let me take on your problems
like their my own.

I'm only truly happy when I'm with my niggas doing
hood rat shit or writing poetry.
I wanna get on stages and let people find me relatable.
I want to not relate to people.

I'm one year away from 18 and my mom says
learning things and making mistakes are a part of being an adult,
but I don't wanna be an adult.

I just wanna have my shit together.

Battle

My mother says that I am
the only aspect of my father's life
that he cannot control.
I figure this is where his anger comes from.
Our interactions have gotten so bad
that I do not react when he calls me out my name.
He says, "Bitch!" and I go from a forest fire
to the quiet stream interweaving a mountain.
He says, "You little disrespectful nigga!"
and my subconscious transports me somewhere
away from all of this.
I have never been a stranger to defending myself
but I've also
never been at war
for this long.

When I realized I had been assaulted
I never wanted to speak about it
Because it seemed like in being a girl,
it wasn't a matter of *if* it happened
but *when*.

I did not want to be another statistic.

shots fired

my parents have hated each
other my entire life.
therefore,
I've always wondered if
there's a part of them
that hates a part of me.

when I'd make my
mother angry as a child,
she'd contort her face into a
look of disgust and say,
"You sound just like yo daddy!"
and this was her biggest insult.
a shot at me?
or my father?

it was the weirdest thing to argue against as a child.
I didn't even know what I was supposed to be mad at
but I felt the fury balled into my fists
and furrowed in my brows.

"I'm sorry that I sound like my other half?"
"I'm sorry that he is my father?"
"I'm sorry that you chose to have a child with him?"

it felt wrong to be offended by this.
but when my mother is angry,
her insults shoot for the stars.
she wants the last laugh
and will dig up however much dirt to get it.

I was in the middle of laughing at something when my father
stops what he's doing to stare at me blankly.
he says, "You sound just like yo mama."
and I feel the weight of their trauma all over again.

it's hard to look into the eyes of someone
and know that they are seeing someone else.

I've spent my life standing in the middle of a gun range.
at first they were shooting at each other
but amid the chaos,
they started shooting me to affect the other.

neither of them have looked into my eyes and complimented me
based on something that reminds them of the other person.
I didn't realize how healing that would have been until now.

I won't say that there was never any love here,
but I will acknowledge that these Soul bonds are oozing with karma
and I've been caught in the crossfire.

will I always be to blame for my parents' mistakes?
will I always be a mirror?
one look into my eyes and they remember that they
were just babies having a baby.

the middle son of a well-off family
and the eldest daughter in a low income household.

both products of their environment
both trying their best
but struggling to get it quite right.

Tokophobia

I am 12 when the boy I love touches my yoni for the first time
It feels like spring
Like soft fingers slowly cascading around a rose in full bloom
I want him to go deeper
to get on his knees
But I am afraid to enjoy the pleasure
To take charge
To say, "Right there," and "Don't stop."

My mother says she gave me the sex talk,
but it was more of an awkward question and answer.
An elusive conversation filled with tight smiles and rigid posture.
I don't remember much
but I know I didn't walk away feeling certain
about the power in my pleasure.

No one knows how to talk about sex

In middle school, I had an older black woman
as my Sex Ed teacher
She instilled a fear in me like no other
Her teachings only covered abstinence
and when we did talk about sex,
she emphasized that it only resulted in STDs and pregnancy

As young girls, we had everything to lose and nothing to gain

I am 12 when the boy I love touches my yoni for the first time
It feels like seeing a sky full of stars in the desert
I want him to go deeper
To tell me he loves me
But this fear shocks through my body like lightning
It wakes me out my sleep when I have wet dreams
I am too full of shame to admit that I love when he touches me
so instead of saying *yes*, I say *no*
Society tells me that enjoying pleasure is for *fast ass little girls*
and I was never taught how to find myself in these spaces

No one knows how to talk about sex

I am 9 when the fifth grader on the playground asks me if I want kids
I think for a second and then slowly consider saying, *yes*.
Before I can, she tells me about how painful it is to have them.
I, unaware of how babies are spawn into existence, am shocked.
I loudly declare, "I don't want kids!"
and have not changed my mind since.

I am 9 when I get my period for the first time on the way to Girl Scouts.
I have no idea that the two are connected.
The only thing my subconscious swallowed whole was the short sigh, small smile, and overall look of dread that spread across my mother's face.

Another child being shoved into the hands of adulthood
when she's still wet behind the ears.

And I could blame america
for capitalism pumping hormones into my food
for improper sex ed and porn that's too easy to find
for violent video games and what the weight of comparison
does to the womb of a child

I've consumed enough media to last lifetimes
Eaten enough bullshit to kill me ten times over
Becoming an adult was just realizing that they don't know
what's going on either.
We are all just fumbling for an explanation in the dark
Too ashamed to say how we feel
and too afraid to even admit it to ourselves

And I could tell you that this is why I've never wanted children.
That I fear what this country will do to another brown baby
That I can't stop society from putting a cage around her brain
or a noose around her neck
But despite my ranting,
that is simply not the case.

My fear of pregnancy did not stem from learning that birth is painful.
no
this fear started long ago
In the loins of my ancestor's ancestors.

Upon realizing that the women in my family are afraid
of becoming their mothers

So afraid of looking in the mirror and seeing
the face that raised them,
that they don't look in the mirror at all.

And who am I to pass down that face?
These hands?
My all too familiar voice?
The way I speak loud in quiet spaces
Just like my mother's mother
and her mother's mother.

I am not ready to split myself in half
to give someone a world that I'll never fully understand

I am so afraid of messing up that I won't even try

But let that be a blessing within itself
That I am so aware of where I am
that I cannot help but move with intention

I am proud to say that I will mother many things,
but never a child.

In Praise of Difficult Women
after Karen Karbo

My cousin says that I am a difficult woman.
Therefore,
I wrote a poem in praise of difficult women.

When my uncle shames me for telling
my 14-year-old cousin how to use a tampon,
I realize that he is afraid of periods.

Maybe the blood is what disturbs him.

He panics at the mess it leaves
but then tells me that I have to have kids.
That our bloodline must continue.

He always speaks in hypocrisy.

My uncle is the type to whoop his daughter
and then turn around and tell her
to never let a man put his hands on her.

But I am the one who is difficult.

When my father calls me a *bitch* for disagreeing with him,
I must remember that this is how he likes his women.

submissive
sunny side up
ready to stroke his ego

Any aspect of me that angers him is just a reminder of himself

The men in my family listen better when I am silent
so I never shut the fuck up.

I've had 18 years' worth of pacifism and gaslighting
2 worth of rage and unlearning
And a forever of healing and acceptance

The irony is how they taught me to be everything I am not.
Said to sit up straight and be a young lady.

I couldn't even get comfortable in them hard ass church pews
before someone yelled at me to close my legs.

They taught me that I was the problem.
The reason I'd be raped and assaulted.
And the craziest part is...
they almost had me with that bullshit.

I used to believe that I liked to play with glass.
Fixing broken boys felt like second nature.
I never wanted kids,
but I sure did mother these niggas.
Sure did make space for them to make a home out of me.

The common belief is that girls tend to date boys like their fathers
So am I to blame mine?

The weeping prophet?
The one that convinced me God made woman from man's rib.

As if I didn't fucking come first.
As if I shouldn't always CUM first.

I find it hard to believe that I was only
created for the benefit of someone else.
And I don't need the men in my family to agree.
They only believe the black woman
is the most disrespected person in America
when it comes out a man's mouth
So do you listen better when I am silent?

Do you even listen at all?

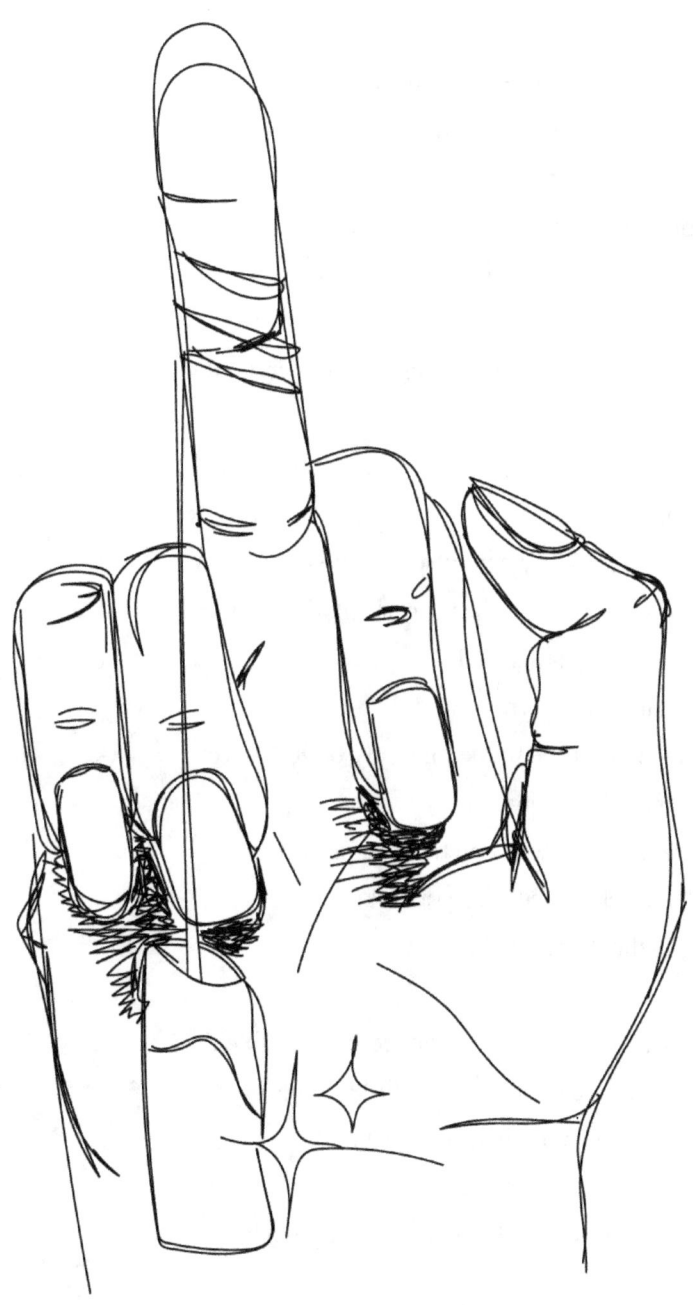

A Happy Poem: Post Breakup

I should have written more happy poems about you.
It wasn't that you didn't deserve them,
it was that I don't write happy poems
and a girl having enough power
to make me do so was terrifying.
I had forgotten what it felt like to write about love.
For so long I've only written about the hurt.
About the abuse.
About the way I win poetry slams writing about the two,

So I think I'd like to try writing about your smile.
Or your hair
Or the way your body convulses when you orgasm.
I love the sound of your heart gradually beating
faster and faster until you do it.
The O your mouth forms
is an image that'll be burned into my brain forever.
I'll be damned if I forget it.
You have always been something to marvel at.
I put Chapstick on only for you to kiss it off
and this is the dumbest shit ever.

Normally I'm quick to get annoyed by stuff like this
but you make me appreciate the little things.
Like the color of your hair in the sun.
Or waking up in your arms.
How no matter what, I know I'm exactly where
I'm meant to be.

Things I cannot forget:

The way she looked at me
after our first kiss.

It was the first time I realized that
I have power over someone.

the healer needs sleep

i hear that death is a sweet release
so when i ascend from this dimension,
i won't mind if you don't remember me.

any aspect of my being
that wants to be the heroine of your story is just my ego.

i would say don't listen to her…
but most times she has something important to say;
mostly about me and my insecurities.
the person i am in this reality is stuck between
participating in the matrix,
and isolating herself in the forest

for so long, i didn't understand that i could live in harmony with both
and make it work for me.

i have been angry for years
and i could tell you that this anger came from my ancestors.
from childhood trauma
sexual abuse
being born brown
and girl
but those all feel like things i've told myself
to justify staying complacent.

if i have the world to blame the weight does not fall on my shoulders.

i hear that anger is a choice
and that everything is a reflection of me,
but what if i don't like what I'm seeing?

it is so easy to fall down the rabbit hole of self-pity
to wallow at rock-bottom
to get acquainted with the dirt under my nails

i've made space for shame and guilt in my queen size bed.
we rendezvous at 8
pillow talk about our codependency at 9
by 10, we've snuggled underneath false security
in the only partners we've ever known.
in the morning they don't leave
just change shape
i find them in my 9am lemon water
asking if this new health kick is for real for real or for play play

how long till i abandon my desire to heal my body again?
how long till i reintroduce meat and honk at any driver going
5 miles below the speed limit?
you should be panicking all the time and
rushing to fix the slightest inconvenience.

but let the record show that none of this is comfortable,
it is only familiar.
and familiar feels safe to my ego
since change is uncharted territory

I am tired of dancing

When your father calls you a bitch
it's not the type of thing you'll easily forget.

I woke up this morning and
as my thoughts started to roll in
I hear my father snarl to my 13 year old self,
"You a bitch!"

My inner child still trembles at the sound.

His words shot straight into the void that was my subconscious
and I've been festering on it ever since.
I see my father in all the men I've dated.
In the way I roll my eyes
and handle my anger,
all reactive,
no response.
I either light the conversation up in flames
or passively blow the rubble away.
There is no in between.

So thanks for the trauma, dad.
This poem has been writing me for eons.
My father and I have danced this dance in past lifetimes.
No wonder he looks so familiar.

Our grievances have slipped through the
cracks of intergalactic trauma
and sulk behind us like the shadows we hide from.
It won't stop until we face the darkness.

And I'd love to tell you that I am unfazed
but that is a defense mechanism.

I didn't learn from the words my father spoke.
I learned from observing what I did not want to become,
and I guess
for that,

I do thank you.

My Mother Tongue

swallows emotions whole.
Barely tastes them as they go down
The only way they'll ever see the surface
is if she has enough liquid courage
to let them bubble up her throat like bile.
Spit.
Vomit.

You ask me why it is so hard to be vulnerable,
and this is the reason.
The women in my family store trauma in every fiber of their being.
No one knows how to communicate
The truth hides behind passive aggression,
playing victim, Christianity, and Tito's.

In moments of rage, my mother tongue only knows
how to turn up, cut off, or dismiss.
So it makes me wonder...
What do we have ears for if not to listen?
What do we have mouths for if not to express authentically?

It's funny how some women look their children in the eyes
and refuse to see a mirror.
Forget their history of physical and emotional abuse,
enter their 50's and wonder why nobody calls anymore.
The only way people come around
is through coercion or obligation.

My cries for help have fallen on deaf ears,
and those who could hear me spat shame
because they were afraid to scream themselves.

It feels like ancestors got my tongue.
Like somewhere down my lineage, I took a blow to the mouth
and have been trying to find my way back Home ever since.
Like a million women are trying to speak through me
and I wish I could orchestrate a symphony of sirens.
Maybe instead of words, I'll wail into the ocean
Maybe the sea will carry my song to new lands
Maybe the vibration will cause an earthquake and
split the ground in two
Maybe I'll call this the Promised Land.
Maybe I'll call this Home.

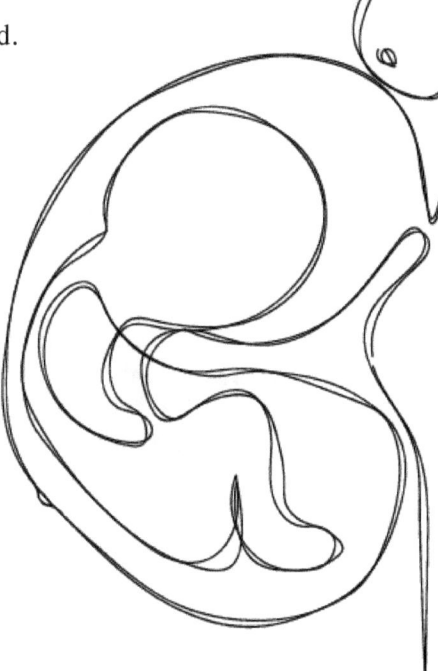

ACT III
ALMIGHTY

No longer am I the victim of my traumas,
I am now the Conqueror of my own healing

take me home

if sand is formed from disintegrated rocks,
what was the desert before a breathtaking landscape?

I like to imagine giant boulders
or the ocean
or the biggest shards of rock that humanity never did see

I hear it was a lush green landscape
filled with people and animals living in harmony
before shifts in the earth's axis and increased temperatures,
it was *The Garden of Eden*

Africa is the Earth's vagina
and I want to go back.
to plant myself into Gaia and sleep beneath her soil
to inhale rich air and have ancient dreams of humanities lineage
and how everything came to be.

I wish we could return to our true being,

because this form keeps me from being
as close to you as I need.

we were once two celestial spirits that could merge into one.
do you remember?

how we split ourselves in two?
the agreement we made?
to occupy a body and learn lessons on this physical plane.

our energy is so thick it is tangible
no wonder I have found you in every lifetime.
no wonder we have found new ways to bask in each other's presence.

even though I miss merging our essence,
how wonderful it is to have a body!

for fingers to move and toes to wiggle
for flavor to dance across your tastebuds
and music to serenade you to sleep

If the deepest I can love you is through this vessel,
then let it be.

we have all of eternity.

In 2006, the International Astronomical Union (IAU) changed its definition of the word *planet*. That same year, the status of Pluto was downgraded so that we could no longer consider it such. Ever since, many scientists have fought to reclaim it a member of our terrestrial planet system.

Pluto
after Olivia Gatwood

Somedays I feel like Pluto.
Drifting alone on the edge of our solar system.
I watch planets pass me by but they don't stay for long.
They never do.

Most days I wonder if I was ever good enough
to have a spot in this popular universe.
Probably not.

I've been hoping that another will come along
and deem me worthy enough to be in theirs.
But it is not that I want to fit in,
it's that I want a place to call my own.

The IAU says to be considered a planet,
I must *clear the neighborhood around my orbit*.
That I must consume or push away objects that cross my path.
Be the dominant gravitational force in my trajectory,
but my biggest flaw has always been pushing
the people I love away.
I don't really wait for an explanation anymore.

When my intuition is off the charts I'm not wrong
and I never have been.

Despite this loneliness
sometimes I appreciate the 3.2 billion miles
separating me from y'all.

Separating me from the nearest human
whose only intentions are to hurt me.

I am far as fuck from the sun
so the little light I do get has never been enough to
nourish the life growing inside of me.
Pluto does not tilt on an axis,
which means that there is always a part
covered in complete darkness.
And, I can relate.

But can't we all?

The IAU says the best they can do is consider me a dwarf planet.
It is a fact that Pluto has been shrinking in size
ever since its discovery in 1930.
It has now become smaller than its moon.
The anxiety makes me walk fast,
I've been so busy trying to keep up with y'all
that I've left myself behind in the process.
My days count as 6 of Earth's
but I still feel like I'm losing time.
The IAU says I gotta do better.
Says I need to meet protocol.
That I must fit all these requirements to make me worthy
of being in this universe.
But these are the same niggas who used to think every
planet in this solar system revolved around Earth.

Which is to say,
y'all have got your shit wrong once and
you are bound to do it again.

Just because I am at the edge of this galaxy
doesn't mean I'm not worthy of all the space I take up.
Despite the challenges I may face on my orbit around the sun
I am here

And I am doing just fucking fine.

Women Who Run With the Wolves
After Clarissa Pinkola Estes

Clarissa tells me the story of *La Loba*.
That to sing is to use the Soul's voice.
And she, made of weathered hands and tousled hair
reminds me of what it means to be feral.
Not many of us were raised conscious that we are free women.
The whispers of our intuition get drowned out
by the demands of this patriarchal world.
With every chain I break,
someone is there to tell me I am being too loud.

Clarissa studies the behavior of wolves
Tells me that to be feral,
one must start in her rightful wild mind
only to be captured and domesticated.
When she returns to her fierce nature,
it is without all instincts
and intuition.

Every woman has felt herself
go missing.
Has searched for her inner child in
the dark.
Tickled the underbelly of her vices and
considered rock bottom to be
more comfy than the ladder.

While captivity is often found in the spaces we thought were safe,
freedom will ask you to jump off the highest cliff into the abyss

If and when woman claws out of domestication,
she comes to the painful reality that she must
relearn all she knew before.
So ask yourself, *do I trust the unknown?*
Or will I continue to argue for my limitations?
Will I push away what is hidden?
Or will I force myself to live a life of loathe?

Clarissa tells me to fuck being nice
That intuition lies within *mis ovarios*
That our human mind has questions
our limitless Soul knows all the answers to.
That if something is deemed unladylike,
do it bigger, louder, and better than ever!

La Loba sings over the bones of a girl who thinks she wants to die,
and suddenly I can breathe underwater.
La Loba runs her calloused hands through the hair of a girl
who looks just like her and suddenly, everyone is a reflection of me.

I am tired of digging into the soil to find life when it is all around me.
The dirt under my nails signifies Triumph.
The blood I lay in is testament to an old life lost,
and a new one that is ready to live.

The siren sings a "scary" song

even amid the noise
i am still
even amid the silence
i am patient
even amid the pain
i am healed
even amid the screams
i know what's blooming inside me
i am the answer

so come play with me
there's so much you haven't seen
come lay with me
I know exactly what you dream

the surface
is a distraction
close your eyes
and imagine
fall deep into the sea
and come play with me

ode to liberation

I battle the ego in my mind by leading with my intuition. By being my loud, erotic, and colorful self and not caring what people think of it.

I honor my humanity so much to the point where I don't feel the need to hide many aspects of myself. I have a curvaceous body that I love to dance in and show off. A mouth meant for eating and inhaling whatever I desire. A Yoni meant for energetic release and pleasure. A clitoris designed for sexual expression and hedonist desires. I use my hands for writing and touching myself. I use my tongue to lick up sweet spills and the sweat off my lover's neck. My hips love to be grabbed and my ass loves to be smacked. I've experienced being caught between a man's teeth and having to claw my way out before he bit down.

I'd prefer we no longer speak of these events as though they are once in a lifetime. Trauma knows everyone's full name, age, and every place you've ever laid your head at night. None of us have escaped her grasp without a dent in our Psyche.

It is a long road to living your life as though no one is watching,
but my God,
I am getting closer and closer everyday.

my yoni wants

to be picky
wants to be wined and dined
taken on long walks where she's asked
a million questions about herself

my yoni wants to be handled with care
stared at in awe
she needs to feel your appreciation
before I can even take my panties off

the last thing you reach
as you explore your way
around my whole body

and rushing will never be an option
for reaching the treasure is always fun,
but the journey is what matters most

I have many Xs that mark many spots
and it will take patience for me to reach my top

I want to do breathwork with you

        I want you to say my name with a smile on your face

                I want you to sing to my pussy

I've had many lovers
that I can't even call lovers
they were more like *thrusters*
men only worried about finishing
as soon as they began

so now my yoni requires worship
praise
to feel good on bad days
she is to be sought out until she is found ready

and pulsing

and in full bloom

Anatomy

Before
I would've tried to ignore the blood
Never acknowledge "that time of the month"
Hide the mess I make
Push you away

Before
I would have asked for you
to understand the blood
But now
it is a requirement
This bleed ain't up for debate

Any part of you that is uncomfortable
with the mess I make
is not ready for a grown woman

My Yoni cannot fathom how there was ever a time
you'd get to slip and slide in all her glory
and not understand how she gets that way

All the glands and crevices that make her
flow a river of sweetness
The tissues and nerves that orchestrate
a symphony of moans
The neural pathways that dance across
my brain to manifest an orgasm

I take pussy power to a whole new level
Stare at my naked body in the mirror
Open my legs and greet a goddess
She says, *Man wants you to fear me.*
Wants you to shun me into oblivion.
Discredit the power that lies between your legs
and hold onto generational tension.

You must release, my love
You must relax into your temple
and exhale any darkness that wants
to dim your light.

From now on,
the only thing you must
hold on tight to
is yourself.

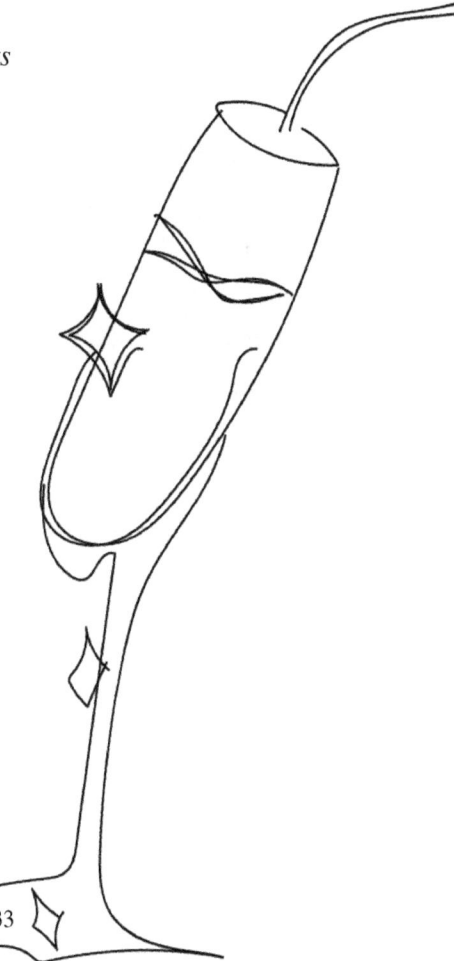

she says I'm like water

flow a river of tears down your face
the first thing you reach for in the morning
sprout life into the seeds that feed your needs

she says I'm like water

that everyone needs me,
but I could do without them
without the misuse and abuse
bottling up my glory and selling it for profit
as if I don't fall out the sky for free

she says I don't have boundaries

flow where I want and fuck how you feel
seep into your carpet
splash out the sink
rain on your parade

she says I am everywhere

that some days she prays for me
and others she wishes I'd go away
that I can't keep secrets
hates that when you stare into my ocean
you will always see a true reflection
staring back at you
some people spend their whole lives avoiding the mirror
but if you were without me for long enough,
I'd be the only thing you crave

I am water

and I don't need her to remind me
everything is either
made up
made with
or made in my image
the moon controls the tides and together,
we orchestrate a beautiful symphony
Together
we make the world go round'

The only time I've felt the holy ghost was at a concert

music has always equated to freedom.
a plane ride to dimensions both within our internal being
and outside our 3D understanding

so never ask yourself how
or why
just move and feel

for any question has unlimited answers
and you may never be satisfied with any.
so here is a series of love poems dedicated to
every concert I've ever attended
and every artist I've ever loved.

One

I am 11 years old and Mindless Behavior has come to the Fox Theatre. Me, the girl they sing about in all their songs, is determined. For what you may ask? I don't fucking know, but I was determined. To be noticed? Brought on stage? Stuck into one of their suitcases to live on the tour bus? It didn't matter.

I screamed every lyric and danced to every song from the top balcony in those tight ass seats. My neighbors hated me but I'm sure the mom and daughter in the seats ahead hated me even more. As I gyrated and went hoarse in the throat, I kept leaning over them as if I wanted to throw myself off the balcony and into Roc Royal's arms.
My body has never shied away from the energy that music brings it. There was no side eye or camera flash that could keep me from moving. In fact, I often found myself looking at other girls trying to be cute by slowly rocking side to side and wonder:
What the fuck is wrong with them?!

Two

I am 15 when I crowd surf for the first time at a Beartooth concert. The music was so fucking loud that I could be standing still but my bones would shake regardless. I entered my first mosh pit and screamed with joy as the white boys rallied up all their teen angst and ran in a circle around me.

I am a natural thrill seeker. So when two giant, heavily tatted white men leaned down to ask, "DO YOU WANT TO SURF!?" I eagerly screamed, "YES!" and together, they grabbed my 4'11" body and flung me to the front of the crowd. No one knew I was coming, so after colliding with various heads, I almost went down. But that night, the audience was united by our love for heavy metal and being outcasts in our small corner of the world.

Together, they lifted me up and happily became the wave I surfed to come face to face with Beartooth. Together, we raged as though the night would never end.

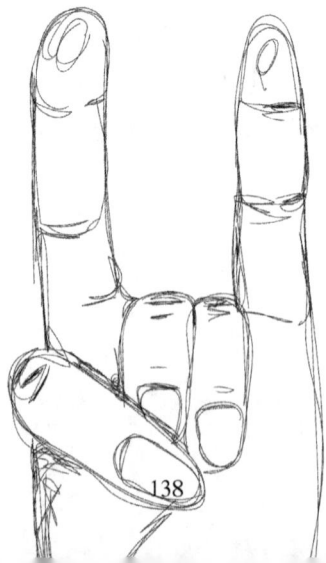

Three

I have just turned 16. Halsey's Badlands Tour has come to my city and I'm ready to wear my shortest pink skirt and tightest choker. I was entering my junior year in High School and her music spoke of all of the things I dreamed about doing with boys who did not love me. I found *La Loba* in a girl with pale blue hair and chanted every song like a prayer:

I'm a wanderess
I'm a one night stand
Don't belong to no city
Don't belong to no man
I'm the violence in the pouring rain
I'm a hurricane

Halsey came into my life right as I was walked into the crossroads of exploring my sexuality and turning my sadness into rage. She made me embrace being a horny teen with daddy issues and a resting bitch face. I fit the aesthetic of the quiet girl gone bad. All of my poems were about feminism and wanting to escape myself. She made love sound pretty and aesthetically painful. All the boys I threw myself in front of were trains going full speed and something in me needed the thrill. They'd sneak me out my window to smoke weed and have sex in the backseats of their Honda Civics. And I knew the experiences would be something I'd forever write poetry about.

Four

I am standing in line at a Juice WRLD concert when the white guy behind me drunkenly runs his finger across my back tattoo. When I turn around, his sober friend stares at me coldly with no desire to come to my defense. The drunk one slurs, "I like yur tattoo." And me, not knowing what I did wrong,

or that at 4'11" I could take up so much space,

or how to react when a man touches me,

uncomfortably says, "... thanks."

The evening progresses with shitty security guards keeping me from the front row and a whole lot of white people screaming nigga. It didn't keep me from dancing hard or forever loving his music, but I never went to a Juice WRLD concert again.

Five

Pierce the Veil will always be my first love. A catalyst in my self development. Every concert served as a reminder that, no matter the trial, I am never alone.

Freedom has always been my top priority, and these were the spaces that ignited my flame. My passion. My reclamation of self.
Here is where I shed my skin, kiss a stranger, and speak in tongues.

I've never felt the holy ghost at church -
but what makes this place not one?

Don't we congregate?
Don't we sing our holy songs?
Don't we leave this place reborn.

If looks could kill

I've executed a million men
call me Murderess
Dawn of the Dead
tell them I don't want their love
just the head

I've wasted my breath on mere mortals
afraid of their own power before
the men lined outside my door stand tall in their armor
but all I see are little boys playing dress up
don't they know I will eat them
will break their bones in two

they think loving me will be easy because
they are only ready to love certain parts of me
whatever is easiest for them to digest
they think they can conquer me
can slay the dragon of their wildest dreams
but no

I will not let a man turn my beauty into my problem.
the solution is loving them from afar
so I can love myself up close

when the full moon is high
I allow divine masculines in my presence
unzip clothes to reveal their blessings
douse myself in oil
and hold ceremony on an altar of pleasure

My mother, Lilith
My father, Eros
so you can call me Monstress
Succubus
the Nymph in nymphomaniac
but I beg you to tell me,
what makes a monster, a monster?

Is it society's perception?
Is it yours?
Is it preserved in her innocence?
Does it lie in her villain origin story?
The reclamation of her eroticism
or the moment she decides to fight back?

Magical Women

Every story I have ever heard about a magical woman
has been tainted by a man's perspective

Eve
starred in a role as old as time
The epitome of a naive woman

Man's first mistake
was claiming she came from his rib
Thus everything she did after was
tainted in his image

Spoke to the serpent
Bit the juiciest fruit off
the smartest tree
They forgot to mention
the serpent represents divine feminine energy
But you see no biblical stories highlighting the
essence of a woman
She only represents the fall of man

This was their first mistake,
to try and convince us that woman did not know everything.

Medusa
worth nothing more than her virginity
Cursed despite how many times she said, "No!"

Another rapist, turns
woman into monster
Punished for being both
beautiful and female

Her womb sheds the blood that should be on his hands

No wonder she turns every man into stone

Before, they wanted her for her beauty
Now they want her power

The story ends beheaded at the stake
Her body discarded and her head,
a weapon of mass destruction

One look into her dead eyes
and a million men turn to stone

Even in death, she could not find peace.

The Sirens
casted villain in every epic they stared in

Nothing more dangerous than a beautiful woman
singing in the moonlight

With alluring voices
their songs led sailors to their deaths
Lyrics so enticing
a man would unbecome everything he thought himself to be

Throwing themselves into the icy waters below,
it was as if they'd become passengers in their own bodies

Now let me say this,
I do not believe that these women are evil
I don't even believe that they were highly misunderstood

I know man saw what woman could accomplish without him
and plotted something devious to take it all away.

What a feat it must have been

to build up a world of lies using dirty hands
and weapons of mass destruction.

To try and convince us that God beget the universe
as if The Creator did not have a womb to birth life out of.

ripe

I bear flesh from the sweetest fruit you will ever taste
so wash your hands
say your grace

there is an art to always being in season
freshly plucked from the soil
ripe and ready to eat

I love enticing you
seeing my juices drip from your chin
watching lustful eyes take in all of me
your lids lower to meet my gaze and suddenly,
I am all that exists

I'd love to tell you my secrets,
but there is nothing to share
woman drips like honey
is portal to the stars
I be maker of all things beauty and pleasure and feel good

what lies between my thighs is something
no mortal man will understand
for me to envelope you in all my grace
is my biggest gift to this planet

I see my reflection within the stars
heed the land I walk on
with every footstep,
I leave a million flowers in my wake
speak to Gaia through the trees and the wind
offer her my blood
yoni to the sun
I am one

god I am

when I die
don't tell the kids I'm in heaven
instead
show them an image of a circle
and point out all the places
that it does not stop
tell them this is what it means to occupy a body

our Soul undergoes different life cycles
and I just so happened to be done with this one
For I am not dead
I am alive in even more aspects than before

there will be no tales about a white man
dying for my vices
no story about the eternal search
for a God outside of me
tell the kids i went into a canal
similar to the one we come out of

tell them
i was greeted by beings I've known for eons
describe
a Vortex filled with colors
never before seen by the human eye

tell them i am both here and somewhere else

the breeze on the back of your neck
the everything on a bagel
all the hairs you shave away
that keep growing back

For I am god.

But do not worship me
for what is God
but not a mirror
of both you and me

I do not dream of an eternal white paradise
filled with those from my past life
that sounds... boring

where is the Soul's progression
if we never learn our lessons
I dream of experiencing all sides of the spectrum
Embodying every archetype that beget the universe
until I exhale new galaxies that beget the universe

for there is so much more to discover
in life after death.

being

i've felt my Soul yearning for the beyond
since i came out of my mother
perhaps that's because the beyond was
where i had just came from

i wanted to turn back
but i knew there was work i needed to do here
and what a cosmic sacrifice,
to know all, but to be told that you don't

i've always had a flair for the dramatic
a way of alluring people into my vortex since June 2000
the courage to put my reputation on the line
the innate desire to embody my most authentic self
to nurture the wounded
to save a life

every time i wandered "too close" to the edge,
the obligation i felt towards family would bring me back
what would they do without their black sheep?
who else to absorb all of their grievances?
it is easy to forget your way when everyone
is so caught up in the illusion

you almost can't help but join the party.

this matrix is structured to hinder intellectual
and spiritual progression
to make you afraid
i've lived a life of preachers telling me who to love
peers telling me who to hate

the weight of this dimension has,
at times,
been too much for me to carry,
but i've never sat it down
never stopped fighting to be in love
with the present moment.

i came back to heal
to learn and experience
to raise the vibration of the planet
and when this body feels dense,
i return to the breath and remember
all i need is inside of me.

ALTERNATIVE WORDS FOR SEX

Worship
> verb
>> to show reverence and adoration for a deity

Touch me in the holiest of ways and together, we will call this communion. Let our bodies be the bread and our juices be the wine. Drink me until you are full. Eat me until you cannot take it anymore.

Didn't you know?

This is *confess your sins and ask for forgiveness* pussy.

This that revelation pussy.

I want you to pull my hair and lay me on an altar of divinity. Bring your talisman. Douse me in oil. Kneel at the pulpit. Together the kundalini rises, the chakras align, and the choir orchestrates a symphony of moans.

Church is not bound by the laws of gravity. Magic exists everywhere. Some of my highest forms of meditation have been in the presence of an orgasm.

I let it ring in the ethers
Manifest my desired reality

My being is a temple where you are only
allowed to speak in tongues.

Lick me until you reach my gooey center.

Melt on me like honey, I am sticky with my love

Don't got time for anything but ceremony

we love soft like satin

like its the end of the fucking world

Eons

Just in case you forgot,
we are a star in someone else's galaxy
Aliens from another planet
The embodied duality of 3D matter and God.

I used to want to understand everything
The beginning, the end, and all that came between
I'd love to tell you a tale where I have all the answers,
but to say that I don't brings me so much more joy.

Even amid all this noise, I am still
I don't offer up my perception for you to alter
or digest an opinion that is projection
It is so easy to only think of this 3D body as dense.
We walk around believing that we are made to consume
all this media
all this rhetoric
but once you turn on, tune in, drop out
you can't help but remember that we are God
nothing is off-limits
and there are not as many rules as you think

my ego is unbecoming

unfurling
unwinding

the spindle that spun
my creation of self
fell off the shelf
and down into the abyss

my ego is the small green blob
occupying a dark corner in my brain
it sits behind a curtain
and shouts my fears all day

the day i pulled
the curtain back
I had to attack
a fact I never knew
that all these years
the origin of my fears
was never me
it was you

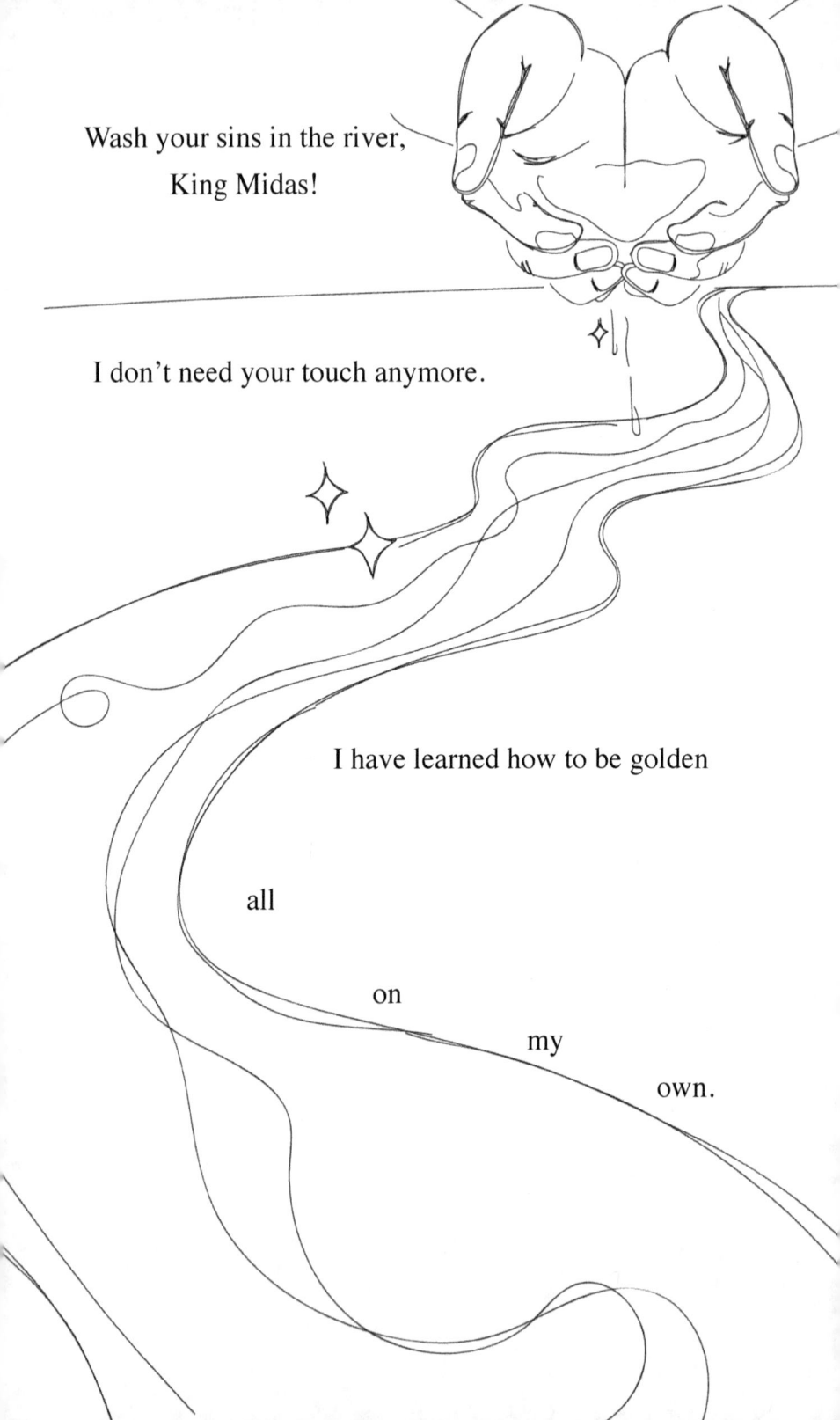

ACKNOWLEDGMENTS

I would like to express my utmost gratitude to everyone who has ever encouraged me to self-publish Brown Girl Almighty.

For years, I hesitated to take this step due to a limiting belief that I wouldn't be able to reach a wider audience. I spent a long time waiting for a publishing company to recognize the power of my words, without realizing that I was the one standing in my own way.

However, I acknowledge that everything happens in divine timing, and I truly believe that this book is being published now for a reason. 8 years after its origin, in the year of 8, following Jupiter's transition into Gemini.

I am at a time in my life where I am moving forward and evolving into a better self every day. This book is the release of old versions of self and a tool for forgiveness. Therefore, I deeply thank those who have hurt me and apologize to those I have hurt. I understand soul bonds and karma, and have alchemized my pain into freedom.

I've been lucky to work with an incredible team to assist with the birth Brown Girl Almighty.

Thank you to Hausson for your editing skills, pep talks, and helping me understand the weight of my words.

Thank you to Cori for your incredible illustrations and graphic design work for Brown Girl the Brand.

I am immensely grateful to Venissa for being the perfect cover model to embody brown girls everywhere and to Dajzha, for your exceptional photography.

Lastly, I express my deepest appreciation to all of my YouTube subscribers. You all have believed in Brown Girl Almighty for the longest and I am ecstatic that you finally get to have a copy of your own.

In full gratitude,
Trinity

PHOTO © JONATHAN JONES

I am Trinity.

Gemini loudmouth poet who speaks first and thinks later. I am funny as fuck and love holding conversations and engaging with others. I am a healer by nature and have always found the most unique ways to express myself. I am a traveler; vagabond by nature. Being of earth and the cosmos. Divine interpreter of duality and all things symbolic by nature. I give birth to my ancestors' wildest dreams and heed the trajectory of my next lifetime. I am the creator of my own reality and powerful as fuck and the word "fuck" does not even equate to how powerful I am. It is more like a word unspoken in modern language. Something only communicated by God and the sound of nature that man has not pillaged.

I am Trinity and I thank you for reading.

Trinity is a poet, youtuber, and holistic healer from Atlanta. She received her education at North Carolina A&T State University, where she reigned as the poet laureate of the 2019 - 2020 school year. After taking a leap of Faith, she dropped out to document her healing journey with psilocybin mushrooms. Her authenticity has taken her far and her passion for creating community has inspired a string of events, ceremonies, and spiritual retreats worldwide. She finds joy in connecting with others and helping them see the world in a new way.

YouTube.com/@etherealtrinity
Instagram: @etherealtrinity + @browngirlalmighty
TikTok: @etherealtrinity + @browngirlalmighty

www.ingramcontent.com/pod-product-compliance
Lightning Source LLC
LaVergne TN
LVHW010326070526
838199LV00065B/5666